Your Family History

Your Family History:
A Handbook for Research and Writing

by
David E. Kyvig
University of Akron
and
Myron A. Marty
St. Louis Community College at Florissant Valley

AHM Publishing Corporation
Arlington Heights, Illinois 60004

ACKNOWLEDGMENT

The authors gratefully acknowledge the assistance of many individuals and institutions in the preparation of this handbook.

The University of Akron American History Research Center, the Louisiana State University Department of Archives and Manuscripts, and the Family History Files at Florissant Valley Community College supplied excerpts from family histories. In each case, names were changed to preserve the privacy of the author and his or her family. The excerpts on pages 17, 55, and 64 came with permission, from Sandra Skrien, "Ole Johnson Skrien: A Norwegian Immigrant in the 1870's," *North Dakota History* 43 (Winter, 1976), pp. 32-35; the copyright is held by the State Historical Society of North Dakota.

Photographs were provided by Anna Buelow, Russell Golly, H. Roger Grant, Eleanor Heishman, David Jackson, Frances Kuhl, Eleanor and Elvera Kunz, Louise Marty, Roy and Glenna Plunk, Willie Oats, and Cynthia Ragan. Other photographs came from the files of the Bureau of Agricultural Economics, Record Group 83, National Archives and Records Service; the Summit County, Ohio, Historical Society; and the University of Akron American History Research Center.

Rick J. Ashton, David H. Culbert, Mark Friedberger, H. Roger Grant, Jeanette Lauer, Arthur S. Link, Shirley Marty, Daniel Nelson, and Thomas J. Schlereth read various drafts of the manuscript and offered many useful suggestions. The authors, nevertheless, bear full responsibility for everything they have written.

CONTENTS

Cemetery headstones often provide birth and death dates, though they are seldom as rich in information as these. Here a man lies between his two wives, both of whom he outlived. Neither woman reached her eighteenth birthday, and the man died at twenty-five. The second wife died after childbirth and was soon followed by her infant daughter. The elaborate carving hints that the family was financially well-to-do.

Every family has a story of its own. Its roots are distinctive. Its pattern of customs and traditions is unduplicated. A family history tells a story of a family, capturing its experiences through changing times and places and relating them to people and events encountered through the generations. It describes such things as the family's social and economic situations, living arrangements, religious orientation, internal relations and self-understanding, and geographical migrations. Good times and bad, successes and failures, dreams and disappointments, the unusual and the ordinary—all of these have a place in a family history. Writing a family history is an exciting and rewarding experience for anyone with the ambition to try it.

A family history begins with research into the family's past and present. Research—sometimes an imposing word—is nothing more than a systematic attempt to satisfy curiosity. It makes little sense to undertake a family history simply because someone else thinks that it should be done, but just a little curiosity about one's roots, given a chance, can grow into a strong desire to reconstruct one's family's experiences. Perhaps if you contemplate the benefits of writing a family history, you will decide that it is a worthwhile project for you.

And what are the benefits of writing a family history? First, the writer gains new perspectives on himself or herself. Such perspectives lead to new self-understandings. For example, to a third-generation descendant of European immigrants, reconstruction of the story of a family's coming to America and its experiences here yields insights into the sense of belonging that ties to the old country and its people provide.

Second, a family history offers insights into the times in which the family lived, and shows the role of unheralded people in society. Historians have studied great events and the lives of prominent individuals at length. However, they have only begun to study the lives and experiences of ordinary individuals and families in America. If people throughout the country would write histories of their families, a clearer and more accurate picture of the American past would emerge. (Later in this handbook you will learn how you might deposit your family history in a collection where it will be preserved permanently and made available to qualified researchers.)

Third, on the more immediate level, the story becomes a part of the written record of the family and thus is not only a valuable historical document but also is one to be cherished by a small group of people. Perhaps your account can be part of a larger effort, with other members of the family telling other parts of the story from different vantage points.

Fourth, the author learns a great deal about how history is written, the processes used, and the limits of certainty by gathering, sifting, sorting, and arranging data; analyzing information for its meaning; coping with gaps in the record; and putting everything together to tell a coherent story. In any case, writing a family history can be an interesting and exciting experience, one that stimulates enthusiasm for history as few other endeavors can do.

There is a difference, by the way, between a family history and a genealogy. A genealogy is concerned primarily with lineal descent. Many people have found tracing their genealogy to be a fascinating hobby, and many techniques described here can be used for genealogical research. A family history fleshes out the information found in genealogical charts by placing a family into a broader context and by telling more about family members. A writer of a family history can learn from genealogists the importance of factual accuracy in recording names (including maiden names), dates, places, and so on. Data sheets similar to those used by genealogists are included in this guide. If they are filled in carefully as your research progresses, they will provide useful points of reference when the time comes for writing. Upon completion of the project, they should be removed from the guide and attached to the family history. (You will be fortunate, incidentally, if someone in your family has worked out your genealogy and is willing to share it with you.)

Many families have group pictures taken in front of their home. By observing the background as well as the focus of the picture much can be learned about the family's circumstances. Here is a large clan in which the males have a wide variety of tastes in dress ...

One caution must be raised at this point: Curiosity by itself is not sufficient for undertaking a family history project. One needs sources of information, and if these are too remote from the writer or simply not available, it may be very difficult to complete a family history. Few of us have the resources of Alex Haley, the author of *Roots*, who, in piecing together bits of information about his family, traveled to the African village from which an ancestor had been kidnaped and sold into slavery two hundred years ago. Like any wise researcher, you must consider your opportunities and limitations before deciding whether to proceed with a family history project. But do not give up too easily. You might be surprised at what you can uncover once you begin.

Throughout this handbook are examples of documents, photographs, interviews, and other materials which can be used in preparing a family history. Excerpts from family histories written by college students are also included. These various items illustrate some of the things others have found and written. They should suggest to you a few of the possibilities for discovering and explaining your own family's past.

PURPOSES OF THIS HANDBOOK

Writers of family histories face many questions: What are the potential sources of information? How can they find a focus for their effort? How far into the past should they go? How can they find a good starting point, both for the research and the writing? What kind of questions should they try to answer? How can they most effectively gather useful information? What is relevant and what is irrelevant to their purposes? What kinds of problems are they likely to encounter and what dangers await them? What is "enough"? What is "too much"? This handbook attempts to deal with these and other questions.

If reading this handbook encourages you to decide to go ahead with an attempt to write your family's history, use it for all it is worth, but do not be limited by it. You may have perfectly logical ideas and approaches which have not occurred to others. Your creativity and imagination are unique; use them to satisfy your own curiosity. Write your paper, do what you can to tell the most accurate and complete story possible; and make sure it is *your* story.

GETTING STARTED

When you begin your research, you will probably have in mind what you want to learn from your work and the general shape your family history will take. If so, you will no doubt know where to begin looking for the information you will need. If your purpose and design are not clear, you may find that it is helpful to start by compiling a tentative list of the sources of information available. Additional sources may come to light as you proceed. If you find that written records are sparse, as they are likely to be, you may find living persons to whom you can turn. Most likely they will be parents, grandparents, and great-grandparents, or uncles and aunts or close family friends—people who can provide firsthand information and impressions. In writing a family history you must ascertain at the very beginning if family members will cooperate. Usually they are pleased to be asked when the purpose is explained to them. If possible, arrange to meet them to explain your undertaking. If they live at such a distance that a meeting is impossible, telephone or write to them. Do it immediately, since not every family member will be inclined to answer promptly. Once you are assured of cooperation you are ready to proceed.

When the range of available information has been determined, format options can be considered. A typical and often practical approach is to trace both sides of your family back over several generations. You might consider the lives of two people before marriage, then their marriage, followed by their children's lives until their marriages, and beyond. This plan may be repeated for the other side of the family. You may cover only the parents' and grandparents' generations, or extend much further into the past. In fact, some family histories are biographies of a grandparent or set of grandparents, or accounts of one side of the family over several generations. That leaves a sizable gap, of course, but it still tells a worthwhile story. Similarly, if information on some family members is missing, you should include what you can about them and concentrate on those about whom you can learn more. Perhaps someone else will fill in later what you have missed. Still another approach would be to minimize the specific lineages and to try to tell a story of the movement of the family from past to present. It is important for you to decide as early as possible which of these approaches—or possibly one not mentioned here—you are likely to follow. You should of course reserve the option to shift to another one, if necessary.

Another important concern is focus. There are many alternatives, and one can decide which to follow later, while doing the research and writing. An ethnic focus poses an attractive possibility. If you are a third-generation American, for example, writing about your family, you might ask why your grandparents came to this country, what life was like for them before they came, where they settled when they came to America, what kind of house they lived in, how they made a living, what kind of adjustments or pressures to conform they faced, what customs they brought with them and how these were perpetuated, how they adapted to the English language and American ways of living, and so on. The influence of ethnic background on children of immigrants is also interesting to study. For example, why did some try to hide their ethnic identity? For third-generation Americans there are such questions as: What does being Italian, or Polish, or Irish, or a member of some other ethnic group, mean to you? What traditions have you retained and do you wish to retain? What are the advantages and disadvantages of ethnic affiliations? Member of racial minorities or religious groups will want to ask similar questions.

The economic development of the family offers another possible theme. How did the grandparents and perhaps great-grandparents make a living? What kinds of skills did they possess? How was their economic status reflected in their style of living? How were the lives of their offspring affected by their economic status? What occupational traditions, if any, were continued, and why? How important have economic considerations been in shaping family life? Can the family history be told in terms of steady economic progress and stability, or of alternate prosperity and adversity, or of persistent hardship?

The depression of the 1930s caused distress for many families, while others weathered the crisis without great difficulty. Learning how people lived through those times often helps to explain their behavior, fears, and joys in later years. This student went into great detail describing his grandparents' everyday life and created a vivid picture of their situation.

In the depression years, John did all kinds of part-time jobs in addition to his railroad job just to keep the family fed and clothed – corn husking, wood cutting, loading bales of hay on railroad cars. His main hobby was gardening. The family spent evenings playing cards, popping corn and making taffy.

Lucinda bought a sewing machine at a sale for $4 and made clothes for the kids. There was never enough money to keep them in shoes. Many times cardboard was put in the bottoms after the shoe sole had worn through. The family ate lots of bean soup, mush, cornbread and potato soup. They had a garden to furnish their vegetables. From this garden came vegetables for canning, fruits for making jams and jellies and big cabbage for crocks of sauerkraut. They raised rabbits for meat and a flock of chickens and a few ducks for eggs. Coal oil lamps were used in the evenings to do school work by. The glass globes had to be cleaned each day.

Each fall Lucinda's family got together for a group butchering day for the winter meat supply. John would rub Morton's sugar cure into the hams and shoulders to smoke them. On another day they would all get together and make apple butter.

Decoration Day and the Fourth of July were big days for the children. Usually there were parades and family get togethers, and memorial services were always held at the cemetery.

Their first radio was an Atwater-Kent. Radio became a big part of the family's life during the evening hours. The family gathered around to hear Lowell Thomas give the news, then "Amos and Andy," "Lum and Abner," and for the kids especially, "Little Orphan Annie" and "Jack Armstrong, All-American Boy."

Focus on the educational progress of the family would be closely related. This would stress not only schooling, but also learning that took place outside of schools such as apprenticeships, military training, or "the school of hard knocks." How were decisions about education reached? Was each child treated differently according to birth order, sex, or other criteria, or were all treated alike? What sort of assistance or encouragement did parents provide?

Sometimes an interesting and important story can be told by concentrating on a major experience in a family's history. For instance, that experience might be family life on the farm during the depression of the 1930s, the progress of the family up to that time, the effect of hard times on the future of the family, and the way the family remembered it in later years. The family life of an urban industrial worker or professional person could be treated in similar fashion.

... here a couple and their children in front of their large farm house ...

You might choose to relate the story of the family to the history of the United States. How was the family affected by World Wars I and II, by prohibition, by the depression, by cold war tensions, by the New Frontier and the Great Society, and by the Vietnam war? What were family attitudes toward the Ku Klux Klan, the Scopes trial, the campaign of Al Smith in 1928, Franklin Roosevelt, and the New Deal? Toward McCarthyism, the racial unrest of the 1950s and the 1960s, the Vietnam war protests, and movement for female equality? How did the family react to Watergate, the energy crisis, and other issues?

GATHERING INFORMATION

The need to identify and exploit all the possible sources of pertinent information challenges the ingenuity of researchers and writers. Among the sources of information, you will find that *family records* are extremely useful. Unfortunately, most families do not live with the notion that some day they will be historical subjects. Consequently, they often do not record or retain information that would be useful to later writers. Yet, once one starts digging, there may be surprises in store. Look for diaries, scrapbooks, high school or college yearbooks, old school papers, photo albums, baby books, health records, letters, and boxes of clippings. Old family Bibles often contain at least some some genealogical information. Frequently, if someone saved a document there was a reason for doing so; try to find out why it was thought to be significant.

Vital records, such as birth, marriage, and death certificates are very helpful to family historians. They are available from state or county agencies (usually called bureaus of vital statistics) where the event occurred. *Legal documents* like divorce

...another farm family of the same period but enjoying greater prosperity, judging from the style of dress and the appearance of their home...

decrees, tax records, deeds of trust, property titles, mortgage certificates, and contracts may be found in county courthouses as well as at home. *Church records*, principally baptismal and confirmation certificates, can be useful. If the family has been active in church affairs it might be useful to look more closely at documents in church files, such as parish histories, annual reports (which show officers and members in the organizations), and even minutes of meetings, especially if the persons being investigated held leadership positions. Shortly after the Civil War *city directories* began to be published for many American cities. These comprehensive lists of heads of households normally indicate home addresses and occasionally occupations as well; they can usually be found in local libraries.

Census records, both *state* and *federal*, frequently prove extremely useful in family history research. The federal government has taken a population census every ten years since 1790; researchers can use surviving records through the 1900 census (practically all the 1890 returns were destroyed by fire in 1921). The 1790-1840 returns show only the names of heads of households; other family members are recorded by age and sex. From 1850 onward, the name, age, and state or country of birth of all persons in the household are listed. Each succeeding census expanded the categories of additional information so that by

1880 there are data on birthplace, each parent's birthplace, race, relationship to the head of the household (boarders and servants are identified as well as relatives), occupation, education, and physical disabilities. Until the early twentieth century, some states conducted their own censuses midway between federal enumerations. These surveys often provide more detailed information on education and financial matters than their federal counterparts. Furthermore, unlike the federal census, use of the state censuses is entirely unrestricted.

Your university or public library may have microfilm copies of the federal and state census records you need; if not, the librarian can probably arrange to borrow them for you. The National Archives no longer searches census records on request. Instead, complete microfilm sets of the 1790-1900 federal census returns have been deposited in each of its eleven regional branches. Libraries may borrow whatever microfilm you need from the nearest branch. Since the returns are organized geographically,it is necessary when requesting microfilm to know the state and county in which the person being investigated resided. It is helpful to know the town or township, and, for large cities, the ward. One exception to this general pattern of availability is the 1900 census which, because of concern for the privacy of persons still living, may be examined only at a National Archives branch.

... here a poor family with outdoor plumbing (note the basin on the right end of the porch) and obvious pride in a musical instrument.

Several types of *military records* may prove helpful in learning more about your ancestors, although you need certain information to make use of them. For military volunteers, 1775-1902, the National Archives holds service records which show the person's term of service, rank, and unit, and also often his age, birthplace, and place of enlistment. A search will be conducted for an individual service record if the person's full name, the war in which he served, and the state from which he enlisted can be provided. Other information can possibly aid in the search. If the record is found, copies will be provided and the inquirer billed. Applications for military pensions and records relating to those who served in the regular army may contain even more information. Access to these and other military records is discussed in the pamphlet *Military Service Records in the National Archives of the United States,* available on request from the National Archives, Washington, D. C. 20408.

Unconventional sources often provide important information about family experiences. In this history of her ancestors' separate migrations from Norway to the United States, this student used a humorous tale handed down for several generations to indicate her grandfather's enthusiasm and limited understanding of what he encountered in the new land. Painted on an old trunk was information which supplemented a newspaper account of how other relatives reached Minnesota.

After hearing glowing reports of America, many Norwegian peasants found life in their native land unbearable. Whole families left their towns to head for a land where they could not only advance themselves economically, but where they could also own land, change their occupations if they so desired and have a voice in determining their own government. Too, while many landowners' sons could afford to buy exemption from military service, others less fortunate chose emigration as the alternative.

Although Ole Johannesen Skrio* had served in the Norwegian Army from 1866 to 1871, he still felt the urge to better himself abroad. His story begins on May 5, 1874, in Bergen, Norway, where he departed his homeland and parents, neither of whom he would see again.

The only stop made on the way across the Atlantic was in England, where, as a memento of this layover, Ole bought a Sheffield razor. When the SS Harold Haasfagen docked in the port of New York on May 26, 1874, half of the journey was over. Ole delighted in telling how he "met" America. "At last," he thought, "I've arrived in this beautiful, bountiful land of opportunity." When he saw a cart with the most sumptuous red apples on it, he took it as an indication of what a wonderful place this country was and how bright his future was. After being at sea for three weeks, the apple was appealing, not only as a "sign," but also as food. As he sunk his teeth into it, it became soft, and squishy and juice ran down his arms. "I hope this isn't a sign of what America will mean to me," he often quoted himself as having said. He took it back to the vendor and complained loudly that the apple that looked so perfect on the outside was just plain rotten on the inside. "But that's a tomato!" he was told.

Kari Sanden Skrien, Ole's wife, later spoke of her trip from Norway on a sailing vessel. She, her father and mother and five brothers and sisters left in 1871, anticipating a relatively short journey. Due to strong headwinds, the trip took 13 weeks and provisions ran dangerously low. Finally, the food was divided equally among the passengers so that they themselves would know just how much was left. Toward the middle of the ocean whales in great numbers began to follow the ship. In order to keep

---

*It was the practice of the Norwegians to add "sen" to their father's name, in order to have a surname. Ole Johannesen (son of Johannes Olsen) used five different names formally on legal documents, adding the Skrio, or later, Skrien, because there were so many Johnsons or Johannesens in America. The name Skrien comes from the word "landslide," which was the area that Ole was from in Hallingdal, Norway.

them from capsizing the ship, the immigrants threw bits of food overboard, and after three days the large mammals moved on.

While we have no description of the route Ole took to Iowa, the obituary of his mother-in-law tells of the last leg of a journey three years earlier. Ole's trip was probably much the same. "After arriving in Albert Lea," the story goes, "they walked the entire distance to the home of Tosten Groe in Silver Lake Township ... Mrs. Sanden has often told of the trip from Albert Lea (30 miles) afoot with Mother and Father and all [six] children carrying some part of their household possessions." The trunk which the Sandens carried has the family's name and routing painted on the front: "Asle Olsen Sanden LaCrosse Albert Lea Vort Conty Min Nord Ame."

World War I selective service records are a little known but quite valuable source of family information. All resident males between eighteen and forty-five years of age were required to register for the draft. Some twenty-four million registration cards—containing information on the registrant's birth date, race, citizenship, occupation, employer, nearest relative, and physical characteristics (covering almost every male born between 1873 and 1900)—are arranged by state, county, and draft board. These are stored at the Federal Records Center in East Point, Georgia 30044. Staff archivists will conduct a search for an individual registration card if they are provided with a name, birth date, and location (at least the county in which the person resided, and preferably a street address, especially for large cities). If the proper card is found, you will be sent a modest bill, and upon receipt of payment, a photocopy of the registration card will be mailed to you. Although these files contain only the names of males in a certain age range, they represent the largest single unrestricted body of information on individuals after the 1880 census and may prove to be very helpful to you.

Do not overlook sources of information that are not in written or printed form. Useful artifacts include letters and ribbons won in high school or college sports, trunks (which might possibly have lettered on them the itineraries of immigrants who brought their earthly possessions to America in them), dishes, jewelry, mementoes and awards (like service pins or plaques), trophies, military or other uniforms, tools, and keepsakes found in old treasure boxes. There may be a good story in an old bicycle or a baseball glove. If you look for significance in such artifacts, you will become more sensitive to the material environment in which your family lived. Many of these artifacts have little monetary value, but, carefully considered, may reveal priceless information about family members. Cemetery headstones are often overlooked as possible sources of birth and death dates.

Photographs also can be among the best sources of information about a family. Not only can they show what family members looked like, but also they can reveal much about the family's activities, economic situation, and personal relationships. Examine photographs carefully, the background as well as the

Form 1

REGISTRATION CARD No. 13

1. Name in full *Alfonse* (Given name) *Capone* (Family name) Age, in yrs. 21

2. Home address 2216 *Arctic* (No.) (Street) *Atlantic City* (City) *N.J.*

3. Date of birth *January* (Month) *17* (Day) *1896* (Year)

4. Are you (1) a natural-born citizen, (2) a naturalized citizen, (3) an alien, (4) or have you declared your intention (specify which)? *alien*

5. Where were you born? *Montella* (Town) *Avellino* (State) *Italy*

6. If not a citizen, of what country are you a citizen or subject? *Italy*

7. What is your present trade, occupation, or office? *Butcher – Meat Cutter*

8. By whom employed? *Self*
   Where employed?

9. Have you a father, mother, wife, child under 12, or a sister or brother under 12, solely dependent on you for support (specify which)?

10. Married or single (which)? *Single* Race (specify which)? *Caucasian*

11. What military service have you had? Rank _____ ; branch _____
    years _____ ; Nation or State _____

12. Do you claim exemption from draft (specify grounds)?

I affirm that I have verified above answers and that they are true.

Alfonso Capone
(Signature or mark)

If person is of African descent, tear off this corner

Government records on individuals such as census returns or this World War I draft registration card, can provide a variety of information, some of it unexpected.

center of attention. What family activities, interests, and possessions appear? Are family members always pictured at home, in parks, or other locations within the community, at work, or on vacations? What can you tell about their home life and economic status from the exterior or interior of a family's residence? Does clothing suggest prosperity or poverty, attention to appearance or carelessness? Are nonfamily members frequently part of the scene; if so, who are they? In group pictures, do particular family members, for instance two sisters, always seem close to each other or as far apart as possible? Are family members shown touching one another, perhaps holding hands? Pay attention also to the architecture of the buildings in the pictures. Ask yourself what is distinctive about their styles. Dates on photographs can increase their value, and perhaps the picture itself will contain clues which will allow you to determine its date. A birth or wedding picture is usually easy to date, but also it may be possible by studying photographs to learn such things as when the family acquired its first car or moved to a new residence. As you gather and identify photographs, carefully write captions on the back in pencil so as not to damage these valuable family records. Local historical societies or camera stores can refer you to places where photographs can be copied if negatives are not available.

Not everyone was pleased when families decided to move. In this excerpt, the author has tried to explain how and why her great-grandfather reacted to coming from Germany to America with his daughter's family.

For Johann the trip to America was one of disillusionment. He had left Germany reluctantly and when he saw the cluttered dirty cities and the farms with their grubby fence rows, so unlike his neat clean homeland acres, he felt homesickness that never left him. The family passed through immigration at the Battery in New York, where they found the heat intolerable and the crowds tremendous. From New York the family took a train to Illinois. In Detroit they found themselves without food and Johann decided to get off the train and see what he could find to buy for them to eat. The train porter advised him not to do so because it was Sunday, he was unfamiliar with the area and could not speak English. The porter suggested that Johann give him some money and he would see what was available. Some time later the porter returned with the only food he could find: a rhubarb pie. Johann's reaction was—"It sure smacks good (schmacks gut)!" So rhubarb pie became an American dish loved by the family.

The family settled in Illinois on the farm of their daughter and her husband. They were never to have a home of their own in this new land, nor was Johann destined to own land.

The land was not the only disappointment for Johann. He could not accept a population that was unwilling to work hard to keep everything clean and neat, to keep all weeds out of the crops and fence rows. He was unable to accept the difference in the size of farms in America and Germany which made it an impractical and impossible task. So Johann tried to help his son-in-law by toiling in the endless long rows of corn and wheat. As time passed his homesickness grew, but for Johann there was no reason to go back to Germany where the farm was his brother's. Those he loved were here in America on the prairie of Illinois. And they were happy. One hot summer day, against the wishes of his family, Johann went to work in the fields. By evening he had suffered a severe sunstroke that left him disabled and intensified his longing for home.

Here a young mother living in World War II temporary military housing.

Family portraits can be studied to determine to what extent family members resemble one another as well as how they dressed.

This picture of a Swiss immigrant farmer and his wife was taken in front of their farm home on their fiftieth wedding anniversary. Other pictures of them frequently show "grandma and grandpa" holding hands.

The overlapping of several generations of a family is occasionally documented in a photograph.

Often the most useful information for family history writers is in other people's heads, and the only thing to do is to go after it. Sometimes the desired information can be obtained through *letters*. When writing to seek information, two rules are paramount: First, make your questions as specific as possible. Avoid asking questions like: What was Uncle George like? Ask instead: What did he do for a living? How did he enjoy spending his free time? What was his relationship with his parents? Do not ask a question that would require the writing of a family history to answer.

Jobs held by family members vary a great deal, of course, but in most cases work occupies a very large part of a person's life and is central to an understanding of that individual. This student has made an effort to describe his grandfather's factory job in vivid detail.

In 1910, my grandfather went to work for Firestone, in what is known as "the pit." Work in the pit consisted of heaving huge, red-hot molds from a furnace with a set of three-foot tongs, while another man cracked the mold with a thirty-five pound sledge hammer. The temperature in the shop was often well above a hundred degrees, and men worked stripped to the waist from necessity. The "pit" either broke you physically or conditioned you unbelievably.

Second, make responding to your questions as simple as possible. Leave space after your questions for the answer to be written in. Include a stamped return envelope. Courtesy and appreciation always must be shown. People are more willing to supply information if they are assured that they are providing genuine assistance. Tell them why the information is sought.

If a personal meeting or correspondence is not feasible, a *telephone call* may be an acceptable substitute. Again, courtesy, specificity, and explanation of purpose are essential. It helps to plan ahead, to have questions written out, and to take down the responses as completely as possible.

Conducting face-to-face *interviews* with key sources is the best method of obtaining undocumented information. A very helpful tool in writing a family history is a tape recorder, for it preserves the full interview for use later when the history is being written and eliminates the need to take notes during the conversation. Tape-recorded interviews are themselves objects of historical interest and may be preserved for future generations.* However, long-winded relatives may talk on and on to little purpose, so do not assume that *all* relatives should be recorded or that *every* interview should be on tape.

*The interviewer should seek the written permission of the person being interviewed if a copy of the recording is to be deposited where other researchers might have access to it. For more detailed information on oral history and the use of tape recordings, see Willa K. Baum's *Oral History for the Local Historical Society*, 2nd edition (Nashville: American Association for State and Local History, 1971).

The value of an interview, whether or not it is recorded, increases immeasurably if certain guidelines are observed. An interview requires careful preparation. Adapted appropriately to a wide variety of situations, these guidelines should be useful:

Before the interview

1. Be sure to get in touch with the person to be interviewed in advance, explaining your project carefully and setting a time for a conversation.

2. If possible, gather background information on the person to be interviewed.

3. Outline the main points of interest for your interview. To avoid being trapped in a rigid format, it is best not to write out specific questions. If you choose to write questions out, be prepared to abandon them if the interview takes unexpected but productive turns.

4. If you plan to use a tape recorder, become thoroughly acquainted with its operation, especially the microphone, volume controls, and tape changing procedure. Practice with someone beforehand. If you feel comfortable in the presence of a microphone, so will the person being interviewed.

To get the interview started

1. Situate both yourself and the person being interviewed in a comfortable position. If you use a recorder, place it within your reach but where the interviewee will not be too conscious of it. Try to arrange things to avoid distractions, interruptions, and such background noises as those caused by radios, television, or traffic.

2. Let the recorder run for a few minutes as you chat about matters that are not directly related to the interview. Listen to a minute or two of what you have recorded. This should relax the person being interviewed and permit you to be sure that the recording is picking up at a proper level.

3. Try to carry the conversational style you have established into the interview, encouraging an easy flow between questions and answers.

4. Be sure to check the time and to know the length of your tape so that you will not have to look constantly to see how much recording time remains. Interviews normally should not be scheduled to last more than an hour or at most ninety minutes.

Some tips for conducting the interview

1. Remind yourself that the point of an interview is not to display your knowledge, but to get the person being inter-

GATHERING INFORMATION

Pictures of ancestors at work may be hard to find, but, as in this view of a stone quarry, they give vivid evidence of working conditions.

viewed to tell his or her story. Let him know, of course, that you are well informed, but once you have established that, do not dominate the conversation.

2. Ask questions that require more than a yes or no for an answer.

3. Ask only one question at a time; that is, avoid running questions together.

4. Keep your questions brief and to the point.

5. Start with noncontroversial matters, saving more delicate issues until good rapport has been established.

6. Don't let periods of silence fluster you; the person being interviewed needs time to think.

7. Don't worry about a question that seems clumsily worded. A little fumbling by the interviewer may help to put the other person at ease.

8. Do not break in on a good story because another question has occurred to you or because the person being interviewed has wandered from the planned framework. A valuable remembrance might escape. Try to find gentle ways and the appropriate time for pulling the conversation back on the track.

9. To help the interviewee describe persons, ask about their appearance, then about their personality and character.

10. Remember that persons being interviewed are likely to give a more interesting and vigorous response to a question or statement that implies your uncertainty than one which suggests that you are merely seeking agreement.

11. Try to establish where the person being interviewed was at the time of the events he is describing as well as his role in them.

12. Use the interview to verify information gained from other sources. Do not take issue with accounts even if you believe another version to be more accurate. Be content to elicit as much information as possible. You can decide later which version of a story to accept.

13. When using a tape recorder, try to avoid "off the record" comments; try instead to get the responder to tell you what he wants to tell you in terms that permit it to be part of the record. Avoid turning the machine off and on. Having some irrelevant material on the tape is better than switching off and on again.

14. If at all possible, interviews should be with one person at a time.

Family reunions often generate group portraits. They can also be great opportunities to inquire about the family's past.

15. Remember to aim your questions at getting specific information, but pay attention also to impressions that the person being interviewed is willing to share.
16. Use photographs or documents to encourage people to talk about persons or events in which you are particularly interested, or about which they may have forgotten.

A family's home usually absorbs a significant portion of its income and shapes its way of life. Attention to the physical details of a home or apartment—the space, condition, furnishings, and surrounding neighborhood—can provide many clues to a family's circumstances. Here the author measures the family's material progress and her mother's reduced burdens by describing a home acquired during World War II.

Crestwood Apartments was the home that Josephine found in Baltimore. They were newly-built, government-financed brick apartments. Three bedrooms, a living room, a kitchen, and a bath made up the rooms. A stove and refrigerator were included. It was a luxurious place compared to the mining town houses. The apartment was new and clean, and had an inside bathroom—simply heaven for the family. Since their place was on the first floor, the children could play on the nice green lawn.

Furthermore, there were laundry facilities for the tenants. After years of wringer washers and rinse tubs in the kitchen, and boilers on the stove to heat the water, the laundry room was a true blessing for Josephine. It was in another building, where a list of tenants and the times they could use the laundry room was posted. Each family had a designated time slot, either in the forenoon or afternoon. The family had a specific amount of hours, on a certain weekday, when they could wash clothes. If the mother did not appear during her allocated time, she forfeited her washday for the week. In separate rooms there were clotheslines hung, and hot air was ducted through huge fans to blow dry the clothes. Josephine always liked to be on the afternoon list, since she could leave the clothes hang overnight, until the first women came to wash in the morning.

RESEARCH TECHNIQUES

Certain techniques of researchers are applicable to your methods of gathering and assimilating information. For example, it is a good idea to keep all of your notes on cards of a single size, preferably no smaller than 4 × 6. Allow a margin of about 1 1/2 inches at the right side of the card so that you can write coding information there. This will be helpful to you when the time comes to organize the cards according to the outline you have developed. Use a pen because writing in pencil invites smudging. There is no substitute for neatness and accuracy in recording information. Systematic, careful, and detailed note taking makes later writing much easier.

As you proceed to gather information, remember to make notes also about organizing ideas that might come to you. Research and writing are not independent tasks. You should be thinking from the very beginning about the shape your history might take in its final form.

WHAT QUESTIONS TO ASK

It is impossible to indicate the kinds of information that can go into a family history without presenting long lists of suggestive questions. You should use them as reminders of the *kinds* of questions that can be asked, not as specific questions to be used in every family history project. You may think of other good questions to ask.

It is helpful to think in terms of categories of information when outlining the questions to be pursued. Suggestive questions are presented here within a framework of categories that might be useful to you. The questions you actually ask should of course not be limited by what is suggested here.

Family details

Who was considered to be a member of the family? Is the family conservative? Adventurous? Adaptable? Rigid and conformist? Ambitious? How did the parents meet? How did the grandparents meet? If couples separated, why and how? What was the relative socio-economic status of the partners in the various marriages? What has been the nature of courtships and decisions to marry? Were children born in hospitals or at

The only black family in a small Illinois town were also the town's only barbers. The nature of their business is suggested in this photograph. Notice the ornate interior of the shop as well as the individual shaving mugs.

27

home? Who assisted in childbirth? How have child rearing practices changed through the years? What has been the place of children in the family? At what age was a young person expected to take on adult responsibilities in each of the generations? How have family crises been handled? How have separation, divorce, or death affected the family? What has been the relative regard for men and women? Has the family any dominant figures or superstars? Any members who for one reason or another have been outcasts or embarrassments? What have family reunions been like if they have been held? What were family attitudes toward aging? Who cared for the sick, aged, or dependent family members? Who inherited what?

Personal matters

Describe the physical appearance of various family members (to be accompanied by pictures wherever possible). Were there any recurring physical characteristics (of stature, complexion, or unique features, for example) that made family members similar in appearance? What was the general condition of their health? Did they suffer from any chronic illnesses, disabling injuries, or deformities? What relationship, if any, did the family maintain with a physician or other health services? Were there "home remedies" that were commonly used or passed along through the generations? Did superstitions or old wives' tales play an important part in medical diagnoses and treatments?

Geographical and physical questions

Where has the family lived? Who in the family was first to migrate to the United States or to the community in which it

Clues to relationships among family members may appear in unexpected places, if a researcher is alert. The use of alcoholic beverages and the choice of jobs are common family decisions, but this student has been able to learn some significant things about male and female role differences by examining how the family handled these matters.

Amanda did not smoke or drink alcohol, Ruth does not do so, and her four daughters (and their husbands) abstain from liquor and cigarettes. It is interesting to note that the women were expected to refrain from "those things," while the men in the family could freely indulge. The double standard has carried down through the third generation, since all three of the Patterson's sons both smoke and drink in moderation. Also interesting is the fact that although Amanda suffered much because of Herman's overindulgence in liquor, after his death she still kept a six-pack of beer in her fridge for any sons or sons-in-law who visited. Evidently she felt liquor was the male prerogative, in spite of the problems of her own married life.

Because of Dick's heart condition and illness, Ruth had to become the financial manager of the family. She had not always stayed at home, but worked off and on for a few years in the 1950s when Dick had phlebitis or extra money was needed. Her three oldest daughters also worked before and occasionally after marriage. They were not factory workers, but instead found jobs in a somewhat "feminine" field—as cooks and waitresses in restaurants. Factories were considered as men's domains, and women who worked there (unless absolutely necessary) were rough and unfeminine.

became more permanently located? Who followed? Why were moves undertaken: for health reasons, to change jobs, or to escape unsatisfactory conditions? How were moves made? What kind of difficulties did moving cause? How was the place of origin remembered? What has been the nature of homes (houses, apartments, etc,) and their furnishings? How was sleeping, working, and living space arranged? Who was included in the household? Were there friends, boarders, or servants living with the family? Did married daughters or sons continue to live in their parents' households? Did elderly persons live in their own homes, with their children, in retirement communities, or in old age homes? Did related families live in the same neighborhood or community? How has technology affected the family; that is, when, where, and how did such things as cars, refrigerators, telephones, radios, televisions, and so on, come into the family and what effect did they have?

Economic concerns

How did members of the family earn a living? What were at-

This 1940 picture from Yuba County, California shows some of what can be learned from photographs. Note that despite modest and even primitive housing, most families appear to have automobiles.

titudes toward women working outside of the home? Did family members help each other in obtaining jobs or developing businesses or farms? Specifically, what kinds of work did they do as machine operators, small business proprietors, or farmers? How did their work change through the years, even though they held the same job? What were their relationships with employers? With unions? With other workers, farmers, or business people? How were occupational choices made? What

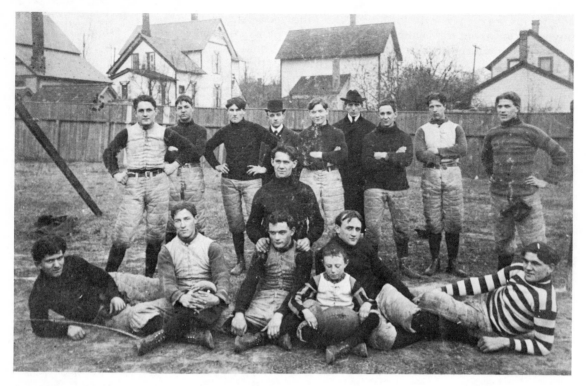

An 1898 picture of a young men's athletic club offers clues about how football was played then and what the neighborhood in which they played looked like.

were reasons for changing jobs? What was their general or evolving economic status? Were all family members expected to bring money home? How were family finances handled? To what age were children supported financially? What was the general outlook on material things? How did the family cope with hard times? Did charity or public assistance (welfare) provide part or all of the family's income? If so, how did the family feel about it? How did family members feel about economic advancement, ambition, and "keeping up with the Joneses?" What was the family's perception of its economic status?

Social and religious practices and outlook

In what kinds of social activities did the family engage? To which churches, voluntary associations, or civic organizations did they belong? What was the extent of their involvement, and what effects did this have? What were their attitudes toward persons of other faiths or ethnic backgrounds? How did they participate in the lives of the communities in which they lived? What were the daily routines of family members? Who were their friends? How were friendships maintained and cultivated? What kinds of family celebrations were held? How did they observe holidays and special occasions? Did the family use alcoholic beverages on festive occasions, routinely, seldom, or not at all? Did this cause problems? What was their attitude toward such matters as race, poverty, and the rich?

Education is one aspect of life which has changed a great deal over the years. Questions about schooling can stir memories and prompt valuable reminiscences, such as happened in this interview.

We lived a mile and a half from church and school, and we had to walk to school. My cousins lived across the creek from us, and we were able to walk together. Time was set for 8:00 to start and invariably they were late, so we always had to wait. That would really provoke me. When the weather was really bad we were taken to school. I remember one year we had quite a cold spell. It remained around 30 to 33 degrees below zero. Then my father and oldest brother rigged up a lumber wagon or box wagon by putting hay on the floor, covered it with a good warm horse blanket and we'd sit on it. Then for the top, to keep the snow off they used more horse blankets and we had a covered wagon. Blankets were also used to cover our legs; rather, we had lap-robes made out of horse's skin. They were very warm.

Our school was a one room school, therefore we had only one teacher. My first teacher's name was Ralph Newman. It was a public school. Our congregation didn't have a school until later, and I attended it three years. There also, only one teacher, and his name was Walter Reese. He usually had around 55 to 60 pupils. We had no grades but were classified by classes. I guess now you would consider it an open classroom for we could answer questions whenever we had a question and answer period regardless of what class we were in. The teacher issued no report cards but had a record book and parents could come and see the record. We had school until July, and on the Fourth of July was our school picnic in the grove near the school. That was a big day. First the pupils presented a program, then came the races. Later a ball game. The mothers served lunch. In the evening as soon as it got dark we had fireworks.

Education

How important was formal education in the life of the family? Did expectations differ for boys and girls? What level of schooling did each family member achieve? What schools did they attend? Did they serve apprenticeships, undergo special training in the military, or obtain other non–school education? If they went to college, in what did they major? What do they remember about their teachers? What part did their education play in their vocations and avocations? Did lack of education impede them? How did they educate themselves informally? What unique skills and abilities did they possess? What attitudes did they show toward those better or less well-educated than they? What kind of encouragement did they offer to younger members who sought schooling? What criteria— financial, occupational, residential, scholarly, social, or educational—did the family set for "success"?

Political attitudes and participation

What were the attitudes of the family toward politics and political parties? How did they feel about various prominent political figures—Woodrow Wilson, Al Smith, Herbert Hoover, Franklin and Eleanor Roosevelt, Huey Long, Harry Truman, Joseph McCarthy, Dwight Eisenhower, the Kennedys, Martin Luther King, Lyndon Johnson, Cesar Chavez, Richard Nixon, George McGovern, Gerald Ford, and Jimmy Carter? What was their political outlook, and how was it shown in their political actions? Were they active in local government? Did they participate in party activities? What party? Did they benefit from being politically active? Which particular political figures or issues—local, state, or national—have had special importance to any members of the family?

The military

What was the nature and extent of military service by members of the family? What were their attitudes toward it? What did they do in wartime? What do they recall about wars through which they have lived, defense plants, attempts to boost martial spirits through propaganda, rationing and price controls, and war bond drives? How did wars disrupt their lives? What ties with military or veteran organizations were maintained after active service ended? What use did they make of the GI Bill and other veterans' benefits? How did their attitudes toward wars and the military change through the years?

Wars often have had an unsettling effect on family life. Notice how World War II changed conditions in the small southern town in which this family lived, and how the family's situation was altered. Also note how the author has used many small details to build up a picture of what everyday life was like in the late 1930s and early 1940s.

As sawmills closed because of both the economic depression and decreasing timber supplies, unemployment levels rose. A government-sponsored program, the Civilian Conservation Corps, paid a dollar for a ten-hour work day, and Isaiah [Bryan] was hired to plant pine seedlings in the Woodworth area south of Alexandria. (He walked fifteen miles to and from work during this period except for the brief time he rented a small house near the CCC headquarters.)

During the thirties, in the small community of McNary, neighbors met weekly for prayer meetings, and on Saturday nights had community plays and "singings." They played dominoes, or "rook," made divinity candy, and listened to Victrola records from mail-order catalog stores. Alice [Bryan] and a friend sometimes worked cross-word puzzles while the men talked [Huey] "Long" politics.

Cooperation was a way of life; Alice did laundry for a neighbor while the neighbor sewed for both families. The men of the community shared such items as "tooth pullers" and shoe lasts, and garden implements and produce. One man even risked his life extinguishing a fire caused by a faulty flue in the wood heater that warmed the small house rented by the Bryans.

The 1940s saw numerous changes in the area, mainly economic. The sprawling complex known as Camp Claiborne, (the army training camp located seven miles north of McNary), brought job opportunities, transportation with its fleet of buses traveling to Oakdale and Alexandria, and entertainment at its theaters and coliseum. Families invited soldiers to their homes for Sunday dinner, and were exposed to customs and ideas alien to their sheltered lives.

Isaiah first worked at the army camp as a carpenter, with his pay starting a $.76 an hour and advancing to $.84 an hour. Family income increased, too, from the rent paid by a soldier and his wife for the one room which they rented from the Bryans. Alice worked as a clerk in the community grocery store, and the oldest daughter worked as a typist at Camp Claiborne.

McNary was a place of convenience during these times. In Glenmora, one mile south, were churches, drug stores, garages, hardware stores, a "five-and-dime" store, a post office and the school. A small medical clinic, two doctors, and a dentist served the community. Alexandria, twenty-five miles north, and Oakdale, twelve miles south, met additional needs.

In this small community with approximately three dozen houses and one grocery store, staples and fresh bread could be purchased, though a loaf of bread by 1942 cost ten cents rather than a nickel. Daily newspapers were brought by bus and purchased by the residents, and mail was delivered on week days by a rural route driver. An ice-man from the plant in Glenmora delivered large ten-cent blocks of ice to the customers' boxes, and a Rapides Parish Book Mobile made weekly visits to the area.

Community customs changed rapidly: as radios became common, and the number of automobiles increased mobility, community "get-togethers" became rare. As the "outer world" was brought into the area, young people were not permitted to walk to Glenmora at night. The many hoboes that had previously been given food at back doors were now unwelcome.

Isaiah continued to work at Camp Claiborne, a short three-mile journey through the pine woods. He also improved the house, including wiring for the electricity that had at last reached this area. No longer were kerosene lamps filled and chimneys cleaned; black smoothing irons became book ends, the radio no longer faded out because of dead batteries, and best of all, deep wells run by electricity permitted indoor plumbing.

In McNary, where most of her childhood was spent, Sybil [Isaiah and Alice's daughter] and friends played on the concrete foundations which remained near the mill ponds of earlier sawmilling days. While their parents planted "victory gardens," they played war games, forming "Junior Commandoes." At the community store they listened to the talk of the maneuvering soldiers from Camp Claiborne. They were given shoulder chevrons and insignias, received "V"-mail, and were taught such songs as "Remember Pearl Harbor."

During these early forties which spanned Sybil's pre-teen and early teen years, the rapidly-changing economy permitted money for entertainment. Groups walked the mile from McNary to Glenmora to view the movie hits of such stars as Betty Grable, Clark Gable, Bob Hope and Bing Crosby. They also enjoyed "shoot-em-ups," "Our Gang" comedies, and the Captain Marvel stories. The battery-operated radio was another source of entertainment, with favorite programs being Red Skelton, Bob Hope, "Fibber McGee and Molly," and "Amos and Andy."

PROBLEMS

Problems in doing a family history will differ with each individual. Obstacles can appear anywhere along the way—at the conceptual, the research, the organizational, and the writing stages. Sometimes information is scarce, sometimes it is abundant. Choices will have to be made, and each choice will set directions that require additional choices.

Probably the most frequently recurring problem will be that of knowing how to generalize, how to simplify reality enough to make sense of it without oversimplifying to the point of creating a false image. There are no easy solutions to this problem. The best way to cope with it probably is to follow your instincts, plunge ahead with the writing, and then read and rewrite what you have written. Implausibility or incompleteness will be evident in most instances. If you ask friends or other members of the family to read what you have written, it may help to protect you against statements unsupported by the evidence. That is possible, of course, only if you can persuade your friends to be critical.

As you immerse yourself in your family's history, you may face another problem that is common to researchers and writers. The time may come, after you have become thoroughly familiar with your information, when you feel that it is not worth going ahead. Everyone knows, you say to yourself, what you are writing. There is nothing new in it. Do not let that notion stymie you. It is probably not true, and if you continue working you will overcome the uneasiness.

Third, you might wonder whether the family you are writing about deserves the attention given to it. Any family is a good

Girls engaged in athletics as well. Look for evidence. This 1929 basketball team played boys' rules long before that became popular. The picture offered a clue to a mother's involvement in high school sports and stimulated her to recall many details.

subject. If your family was wealthy or prominent, you can explore what its members did to acquire its fortune or position and how they influenced society from a position of wealth and prominence. If your family was not among the favored few, their history is equally important. Far less is known about the lives of the poor or the middle class, immigrants, blacks, and other minorities than is known about elite or influential groups. The experiences of such families deserve to be recorded.

A fourth problem lies in maintaining objectivity. It will reveal itself when you approach your sources, whether they are written or verbal, for the sources themselves are not objective. The persons who keep records, and those whom you interview, usually try to cast themselves in the best possible light, conceivably at the expense of others. Detachment will be necessary, especially when it comes to dealing with contradictory or obviously false information. A spirit of skepticism is needed as you separate fact from fiction and sort out truth from imagination. Do not let the kindliness and interest of your sources color your judgement when it comes to evaluating information. Remember also that the memories of those who give you information are selective. Your thoughtful questioning should uncover what they prefer to forget. All that you read and hear must be examined for bias. Here is where it is useful to have more than one account of events.

The problem of objectivity will arise again as you work

through your notes and tapes, seeking to bring your information into manageable form, and later as you write. Some information will please you; some you will find unpleasant. You may encounter touchy subjects such as divorce, suicide, alcoholism, mental illnesses, wayward offspring, family misfits, and other possible embarrassments. Your obligation is to be as frank and accurate as possible, resisting personal preferences which would distort your story. If you are tempted to leave out some sensitive information, ask yourself whether doing so would present a seriously incorrect or incomplete picture of the family. The knowledge that other family members will probably read what you have written may restrain you, but remember that candor is likely to be respected as long as what you write is honest and accurate. Your sympathies no doubt will be revealed, but your fairness must be self-evident. Remember the other side, too. A family history should not be regarded as an exposé or attack on the family.

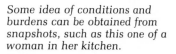

Some idea of conditions and burdens can be obtained from snapshots, such as this one of a woman in her kitchen.

WRITING YOUR FAMILY'S HISTORY

Once you have gathered information and thought about what you have learned, the time has arrived to begin writing a family history. This step is as important as any other, for only clear and accurate presentation of your findings will allow others to share what you have learned. There is no single pattern for writing a family history, any more than there is a single pattern to family life. The information that you have been able to uncover, and the topic on which you have chosen to focus, will strongly influence the way that you go about writing your history. Here are some general suggestions which should make your writing easier and more effective.

Begin by preparing an outline which lists family members or topics in the order to be discussed. One good organizational system begins with the paternal grandfather before marriage, then the paternal grandmother, then their life together, and finally their child (your father) prior to his marriage. At this point, attention shifts to the maternal grandfather, followed by the maternal grandmother, their life together, and their child (your mother) before her marriage. The two lines then can be joined for a discussion of your parents' lives together. This is merely a model, of course; it could be extended to more generations, or altered to suit families which have patterns complicated by divorce or early death and subsequent remarriage. In any case, an outline is necessary in order to bring into manageable form a story that is potentially limitless. A good outline gives the story a cohesiveness and direction not found in something which merely proceeds in an "and then . . . and then . . . and then" style.

Interviews may provide information about customs thought at the time to be so commonplace that they were not recorded. Direct questions can bring out detailed memories. In this interview excerpt, for instance, a woman provides a rich and vivid image of her grandmother's funeral.

Grandma was very frail. The day she died I got to see her in the morning, and she patted my hand. She died early evening. Funerals were different then than now. Grandma was not embalmed. My mother and a neighbor bathed her and dressed her. Next morning they had to go to town and get the casket and wooden box. Friends and neighbors would come to the house to call and the day of the funeral there would be a short service in the home. Neighbors dug the grave. The body was usually taken to the church and cemetery on a spring buggy where the regular services were conducted. At our church they would bury the body first and then have the service in the church.

Later years the undertaker or funeral director would take care of the body, and they had a horse-drawn hearse. Beautiful black ponies. I can remember them so well. When my other grandmother died she had the hearse. Some people had a wake, but it was never done at our house.

The family's history is written by building upon the outline. In the outline, you determine whether to handle your information chronologically, topically, or in some other fashion. As you write, you will provide substance and detail to the structure already decided upon. Be careful to write in good, clear, and direct Engish, avoiding slang expressions and cryptic comments. Keep in mind that your children or grandchildren may wish to read what you have written. They are most likely to comprehend uncomplicated, straightforward sentences and paragraphs which follow logically. They are not likely to understand the "in" phrases of today any more than you understand the jargon of the 1920s or 1940s.

As you write, pay attention to the unusual aspects of your family's history, but do so in a way which avoids sensationalism or overemphasis. Each family's story is distinctive, yet it includes elements which others are likely to have shared. If you concentrate singlemindedly on the uniqueness of the lives you are describing, it will result in an unbalanced and inaccurate story.

Above all, remember that it is *your* project. Teachers and consultants seek to be helpful, but in turning to them, do not let

This picture of a family's church provides information about the denomination, ethnic makeup, and date of origin of a congregation.

them take your story away from you and make it over in their own style. You are the historian, and you will be responsible for the information and interpretations. Few families (none in our acquaintance) consist entirely of saints or geniuses. A claim that your family is so blessed may deny your readers an accurate picture of your family but is not likely to deceive them. Write so that your research is apparent and your judgments, even if unflattering, will be respected as honest and intelligent.

Every family must decide how to use its income, whether it is wealthy, or as in the case of this family, very poor. The student who wrote this recognizd that the details of how income is received and is spent can tell a great deal about family circumstances, decision-making, and values.

For a time in the early 1960s, Walter was drawing unemployment. After awhile the checks stopped and the family had to go on welfare.

Welfare paid the rent and gave the family surplus food. This surplus food consisted of a diet of butter, corned beef, dried milk, beans, raisins, rice, cornmeal, lard, flour and dried eggs. Mary would sometimes sell some of the surplus food for cash. Besides the rent and food, welfare also provided a clothing card to go to Goodwill Industries and get used clothing. For medical care the family had to walk to the clinic at Mercy Hospital. The family had no phone; when Walt's father died in 1962 the police had to come and inform the family. At different times the gas and electric were turned off.

A complete family history ought to contain more than a written narrative. The basic genealogical information concerning the family should be presented in convenient form. The forms included in this handbook were designed for that purpose; they should be filled out neatly in ink, removed from the book, and attached to your paper. In an appendix to the paper, you should list the sources of information used in preparing the family history; at the same time, you may wish to express your appreciation to those who helped you. The use of footnotes is an entirely appropriate means of indicating the sources of particular information as well as of explaining points which do not fit smoothly into the main narrative.

Illustrations will enhance your family history and reinforce its conclusions. Photographs may provide important information as well as reveal what family members looked like. Documents such as diary pages, naturalization papers, school report cards, or letters often enliven your story. Maps can help the reader trace family movement from country to country, city to city, neighborhood to neighborhood, or even house to house within a block. These different kinds of illustrations may be placed at appropriate locations throughout your text, or they may comprise an appendix. In any case, all should be captioned neatly and accurately with full names, exact dates, and other significant information provided whenever possible. When original photographs, documents, or maps are too valuable,

This World War I snapshot provides an impression of an army training camp in San Antonio, Texas, and one way in which recruits spent a spare moment.

Wills can reveal property holdings and sometimes more. This student was able to draw conclusions not only about an ancestor's prosperity, but also about his relationships with his children and their spouses as well.

Throughout the years, even with war and Indian problems, Amos enlarged the farm and prospered, as his will seems to indicate. He left the original plantation to his youngest son Paul and also an additional 152 acres in the same township. Paul was to pay 450 pounds to the other heirs for the land at a rate of fifty pounds per year.

Amos and Elizabeth had seven children, six of whom lived to adulthood. One of their children, Mary, was mentally retarded and lame. In Amos's will he charged his son Paul with keeping not only all the maintenance necessary for his mother but also that of Mary as long as she lived.

One interesting point in Amos's will concerns his daughter Sybil. He charges that she should share and share alike with her brothers in the inheritance, but her share should be held by the executors of the will as long as Harold Stone was her husband. If he died first, she would rightly receive her inheritance. If Harold Stone outlived her, that part of the inheritance would then be equally divided among the other heirs. Harold Stone would receive nothing. One can only speculate on this provision, but it seems that Amos had a strong dislike of his son-in-law. Nevertheless, Harold died in 1774, three years before Amos died. Sybil lived until 1816 so she received her inheritance.

fragile, or rare to be included in your family history, satisfactory copies usually can be obtained. Photographic reproduction provides excellent quality, but it is expensive. The latest xerographic copiers do a respectable job, even on photographs, at low cost.

Finally, your family history will need an identifying title. During the research and writing a natural title might emerge: "Weathering the Depression: A Meteorologist in the 1930s." You might use simply the names of your grandparents: "The Swift and Plodding Families, 1910-1972;" or if you deal with

The family car, especially the first one, often shows up in snapshots. This picture, mounted with a series of others in an album, documents a family driving vacation in the 1920s.

This 1921 Cape May, New Jersey, picture gives an idea of how one midwestern family spent a vacation.

only part of the family you might call it "A History of Otto and Emma Zeitgeist, 1876-1945." The title page should contain the title, your name, and the date on which you completed the family history.

OTHER APPROACHES TO FAMILY HISTORY

Having made the effort to collect records, conduct interviews, organize and analyze information, and write a family history, you may sigh, "Well, that's the end of it." Whether the work was done for a class or completely on your own, it may seem that beyond an instructor or a few family members, no one could be interested in your family's history. You're wrong!

Other people are also exploring the history of the family. By learning from what they have been doing and making your own findings known, you can share in this effort to understand the past more fully.

In recent years, interest in the American family, past and present, has been growing. Many people have undertaken projects such as yours to retrieve their family's genealogy and history. Television has occasionally got beyond the entertainment use of exaggerated comic families. In 1977 the largest audience ever to watch a single program, an estimated eighty million people, saw the final segment of "Roots," the twelve hour program tracing several generations of an Afro-American slave family. There also have been serious examinations of current family life, historical figures in the context of their families, and past societies through the dramatic device of fictitious families. Many scholars have recognized in their books and articles that the study of the family as it has changed over time is important both for its own sake and for what it can reveal about other aspects of society. These various developments reflect an increasingly widespread interest in uncovering the realities of family life.

Leaving home and moving to a distant place, whether another country or a different part of the same land, is a major event in any family's life. This family history discusses the reasons why various members of one Italian family migrated to America, some of the difficulties they encountered, and their continued ties to the old homeland.

Lucy's brother John came to the United States in 1902. Prior to that he had been a soldier in the Italian Army for three years. He came because many young people from his home town came to this country; he thought the opportunities here were better. John came straight to Akron because a friend was already here and working for the rubber companies. John got a job right away at Goodrich in department 25—shoe department. It was the department that all the Italians worked in; the boss was an Italian who could speak both English and his native tongue. After work, John would return to the private home where he boarded with an Italian family.

Peter, the second oldest, came to the United States a year after his brother. He had been working on his family's farm and working for the city, doing road work. On the day he was to leave, his father died, so he stayed in Italy another month. John had sent for Pete, so he also went straight to Akron. John had to promise to see to it that Pete would have a job if he came to the United States. Pete got a job in the same department as John, only working the night shift, and lived with his brother.

Maria, Lucy's mother, thought the world was going to end. Her husband had died, and her two sons had left the country; she was left with only her two young daughters (in order to understand this feeling, you have to understand the importance of sons to an Italian mother—daughters are nice, but a son is special. You can be proud of him, and he'll carry on the family name. It's all tied up with the idea of "family" and it is very strong in the Italian culture).

John and Pete wanted her to come to this country. A friend of the boys visiting people in Italy tried to talk Maria into coming, but she was afraid of crossing the water. Finally John wrote her a letter telling her that if she didn't come to America, she could forget that she had two sons. That was more than she could take, and she sent word that she would leave Italy. John bought the tickets for Maria, Lucy and Rose. "My mother said she wanted to sneak out of town because the older people of the town considered it 'second class' to go to America; only the young people thought it was good. It showed a lack of dignity."

They rode to Naples by autobus. Maria's nephew accompanied the three females. They stayed in Naples for two days in a hotel. It was the first time they saw faucets with running hot and cold water. On September 7, 1907, the three of them boarded the boat bound for America. On September 18, the boat docked at in New York at Ellis Island. They stayed in government barracks there for two or three days. Lucy remembers it being a very nice clean place where she played with a lot of older children. Maria saw a lady selling apples and was confused when she noticed the lady was wearing a hat. Lucy recalls, "Where we came from only wealthy or noble people wore hats and she didn't look very much like either."

The three of them arrived in Akron by train. They wore tags that informed the trainman where the three Italian girls were to get off. At the Akron stop, they were motioned off the train and there was no one there. They weren't expected until the following day. They stood outside for a while, waiting until the station people found a man who spoke Italian. He found out where they were going, he even knew John and Pete, and took them to where they lived. While they were walking through a park, Maria saw a squirrel—she thought it was a rat. "What awful children I have to bring me to this country." Finally they arrived at her son's house and they all started to cry, "Our troubles are over."

The house had three bedrooms—the owner had one, and the other two served the two boys in one, and Maria and the two girls in the other. The kitchen was in the basement, and the sitting room was on the first floor with the owner's bedroom. They lived in this house for one year.

During this time, John got married. Some good friends living in Youngstown had a daughter still in Italy. Maria and John decided she would be a good wife to John. So it was arranged with the family in Youngstown: John would go back to Italy, marry the daughter, then bring her back to Akron; Maria's other daughter, Rose, would marry one of the sons of the man in Youngstown. So John took off to marry his bride—but Rose refused her match. Since Rose refused to marry the son, John was rejected by the daughter when he got to Italy. But he stayed there for a year anyway, and married another girl from his hometown.

Until recently few historians seriously examined the family as a social institution. A World War I three volume impressionistic history by a sociologist[1] and a 1942 doctoral dissertation[2] stood practically alone until midcentury as studies of the structure and function of the American family over extended time periods. During the 1950s, a few historians touched on the family while investigating education, immigration, or colonial business.[3] In 1962 the president of the American Historical Association called American family history "a neglected field,"[4] and seven years later another historian still could write that, with a few exceptions, the situation remained unaltered.[5]

1 Arthur W. Calhoun, *A Social History of the American Family from Colonial Times to the Present* (3 vols., Cleveland, Ohio, 1917-1919).

2 Edmund S. Morgan, *The Puritan Family* (Boston, 1944).

3 Bernard Bailyn, *Education in the Forming of American Society* (Chapel Hill, N. C., 1960); Oscar Handlin, *The Uprooted* (New York, 1951); James B. Hedges, *The Browns of Providence Plantation* (2 vols., Cambridge, Mass., 1952-1968).

4 Carl Bridenbaugh, "The Great Mutation," *American Historical Review*, 68 (January 1963), p.327.

5 Edward N. Saveth, "The Problem of American Family History," *American Quarterly* 21 (Summer 1969), p. 311. Many genealogists, however, had been assembling masses of information while they pursued individual lineages, and their works provided a foundation for much of the current research in the broader dimensions of family history. See Samuel P. Hays, "History and Genealogy: Patterns of Changes and Prospects for Cooperation," *Prologue: The Journal of the National Archives* 7 (Spring 1975, pp. 39-43; Summer 1975, pp.81-84; Fall 1975, pp.187-191).

Historians approach their work differently from sociologists, economists, political scientists, and other scholars of human society. Historians are interested in examining a broad variety of past conditions and phenomena—social, economic, political, cultural, and intellectual—which they regard as interrelated. They especially wish to study the process by which societies change over time. Since information concerning the past, whether distant or recent, comes in many forms and is often biased, obscure, or incomplete, historians have been obliged to employ a wide variety of techniques to learn what they can. Because they refuse to be bound by any particular topical focus or methodological approach, historians have been willing to

A determined black family historian was able to use a great-great aunt's recollections and a few surviving slave plantation documents to discover a number of details about his great-great-grandfather who died in 1917. This ragged but clear photograph was discovered unexpectedly when a sharecropper shanty was being torn down.

ask new questions and to explore nontraditional themes which seem to offer the possibility of gaining a fuller understanding of the past. Not every historian accepts every new approach, of course, and various ways of looking at the past inevitably provoke controversy as they develop. Debate over what actually happened and what it means becomes an exciting and vital aspect of the study of history.

In the past few years, a number of historians have made the family their prime concern. They are among those who have recognized the need to do what has been called "history from the bottom up"—to study usually neglected common folk in order to find out what life was like for most people. A depression or war, for instance, meant very different things to ordinary men and women than it did to presidents, prime ministers, business leaders, diplomats, and generals—the "great white men" upon whom historians frequently concentrated. The family was the primary social institution for most individuals, and thus more and more historians have recognized it as an excellent means for studying non-elite society. Concurrently, rising interest in the history of women brought the realization that their role could not be understood completely without assessing their situation within the family. Developments in the study of urbanization, migration, childhood, education, and the historical implications of psychology also have contributed to an appreciation of the importance of the family in history.

American historians have employed both traditional and innovative methods in exploring the subject of the family. Biographies of individual families appeared with some frequency

A poll tax receipt, a reminder of southern racial discrimination practices, indicates that this man had the political interest and financial means to pay the annual fee to vote. In communities of poor tenant farmers, many did not.

$1.50   POLL TAX RECEIPT   № 1249

COUNTY OF CULLMAN ALA. _____ Jan 5 _____ 190_9_

Received of _____ J M Davis _____

the sum of ONE DOLLAR AND FIFTY CENTS,

for Poll Taxes due by him for 1908:

District No. _67_   Precinct No. _12_   Color _White_

Countersigned by

Wm. W. Brandon
State Auditor.

John J Fowler
Tax Collector.

BROWN PRINTING CO., MONTGOMERY, ALA.

1908

This picture of a family grocery store and tavern shows the owner and his two sons who worked with him (in white shirts), some of their regular customers, some of the items they sold, and, reflected in the store windows, the neighborhood in which they were located.

even before the recent surge of interest, although most focused on individual elite families and ignored the question of whether an isolated family reflected a general pattern.[6] Questions regarding some aspects of family life at particular times have been probed through literary sources, sermons, diaries, letters, and advice books, as well as records of settlement houses, governmental agencies, and other institutions.[7] These rather conventional materials and approaches help to explain facets of

6   F. O. Mathiessen, *The James Family* (New York, 1947); Alden Hatch, *The Wadsworths of the Genesee* (New York, 1959); Ross E. Paulson, *Radicalism and Reform: The Vrooman Family and American Social Thought 1837-1937* (Lexington, Ky., 1968); John T. Waters, Jr., *The Otis Family in Provincial and Revolutionary Massachusetts* (Chapel Hill, N.C., 1968); James P. Baughman, *The Mallorys of Mystic: Six Generations of American Maritime Enterprise* (Middletown, Conn., 1972); and Jack Sheppard, *The Adams Chronicles: Four Generations of Greatness* (Boston, 1976), reflect the range of popular and scholarly works which focus on particular prominent families.

7   Outstanding examples include William E. Bridges, "Family Patterns and Social Values in America, 1825-1875," *American Quarterly* 17 (Spring 1965), pp.3-11; Richard L.

A change of jobs can represent a major shift in the pattern of life as well as the economic circumstances of an individual worker and an entire family. In this excerpt, the author has examined the reasons that his ancestors changed jobs and one of the consequences—his grandparents's first meeting.

Peter, George's father, was a farmer and a stonemason in Clearfield County, Pennsylvania, during the 1890s. As George grew up, the stonemason work faded. Farms were no longer built with large cellars, only small fruit cellars were used, and Peter and his sons did not have enough work. So the boys turned to lumbering and coalmining, besides farming, for occupations.

George eventually turned to coalmining for a livelihood, and worked in the mines around Clearfield County. One such mine was the Berwinsdale Coal Company, where he worked in his later teen-age years. In 1907 there was a bad accident involving another miner named Jasper Simms. A roof slab fell on the man, pinning him to the floor, and his back was broken. George helped carry the nearly dead miner to his farmhouse; the Simms family never called a doctor. Although Jasper was almost fatally injured, he was to heal by himself, without medical care. For several weeks Jasper Simms' life hung in the balance; finally he began to mend, taking several months to fully recuperate. During those months George visited the Simms home many times. But whether he was more interested in Jasper or in his sixteen-year-old daughter, Sally, whom he had met after bringing Jasper home, is hard to say.

American family life, but they do not provide a comprehensive view of the family as it evolved over time.

Less traditional methods have produced encouraging results. After World War II French and English scholars began to develop techniques for studying family history in the absence of letters, diaries, and other sorts of records which historians routinely use. Most families do not keep such records, much less turn them over to researchers. French demographers, interested in population changes, migration, and birth and marriage patterns, used census, court, church, and other records to reconstruct profiles of individual families and then the family patterns over several generations of vast numbers of ordinary people. These "family reconstitution" techniques produce only a limited amount of information about an individual family, but permit quantitative analysis of certain family characteristics. By the mid-1960s some American historians were finding family reconstitution a valuable method, often using it in conjunction with techniques borrowed from anthropology, psychology, and sociology. Quantitative analysis, both of family

Rapson, "The American Child as Seen by British Travelers, 1845-1935," *ibid.* (Fall 1965), pp. 520-534; Ross W. Beales, Jr., "In Search of the Historical Child: Miniature Adulthood and Youth in Colonial New England," *ibid.* 27 (October 1975), pp.379-398; James R. McGovern, "The American Woman's Pre-World War I Freedom in Manners and Morals," *Journal of American History* 55 (September 1968), pp. 315-333; Carrol Smith-Rosenberg and Charles Rosenberg, "The Female Animal: Medical and Biological Views of Woman's Role in Nineteenth Century America," *ibid.* 60 (September 1973), pp. 332-356; Carl Degler, "What Ought To Be and What Was: Women's Sexuality in the Nineteenth Century," *American Historical Review* 79 (December 1974), pp. 1467-1490; and Nancy F. Cott, "Eighteenth Century Family and Social Life Revealed in Massachusetts Divorce Records," *Journal of Social History* 10 (Fall 1976), pp. 20-43. Two valuable collections of source materials are Robert Bremner, ed., *Children and Youth in America: A Documentary History* (2 vols., Cambridge, Mass., 1970-1971) and Robert Manson Myers, ed., *The Children of Pride: A True Story of Georgia and the Civil War* (New Haven, Conn., 1972).

reconstitutions and straight census data, has begun to expose the outlines of the American family's past. Sophisticated quantitative research has enabled historians to begin examining the life cycle of families, the different stages and structures of family life from marriage and early childless years through child-rearing to the spin-off of new families and the return to a childless family. Also, it has become possible to compare the family patterns of different ethnic, racial, economic, religious, and geographical groups.[8]

Much of the scholarly investigation of the American family has concentrated on the colonial period. Both traditional materials and resources for family reconstitutions are available, the total population is relatively small, and many crucial questions—settlement patterns, social structure, economic relationships, and others—revolve around considerations of the family. Impressive studies have traced patterns of family life in individual communities over several generations.[9]

Some school pictures give a good idea of what classrooms were like.

8   Tamara K. Hareven, "The History of the Family as an Interdisciplinary Field," *Journal of Interdisciplinary History* 2 (Autumn 1971), pp. 388-414; Robert V. Wells, "Household Size and Composition in the British Colonies in America, 1675-1775," *ibid.* 4 (Spring 1974), pp. 543-570; Daniel Scott Smith and Michael S. Hindus, "Premarital Pregnancy in America, 1640-1971: An Overview and Interpretation," *ibid.* 5 (Spring 1975), pp. 537-570; Hareven and Maris A Vinovskis, "Marital Fertility, Ethnicity, and Occupation in Urban Families: An Analysis of South Boston and the South End in 1880," *Journal of Social History* 8 (Spring 1975), pp. 69-93; William Harris, "Work and the Family in Black Atlanta, 1880," *ibid.* 9 (Spring 1976), pp. 319-330; Glen H. Elder, Jr., and Richard C. Rockwell, "Marital Timing in Women's Life Patterns," *Journal of Family History* 1 (Autumn 1976), pp. 34-53.

9   John Demos, *A Little Commonwealth: Family Life in Plymouth Colony* (New York, 1970); Philip J. Greven, Jr., *Four Generations: Population, Land, and Family in Colonial Andover, Massachusetts* (Ithaca, N.Y., 1970); Kenneth Lockridge, *A New England Town: The First Hundred Years: Dedham, Massachusetts, 1636-1736* (New York, 1970), and Michael Zuckerman, *Peaceable Kingdoms: New England Towns in the Eighteenth Century* (New York, 1970).

School pictures can be very informative. Note how large this one teacher's class was in 1921. Note also how prominently the flag was displayed. These were mostly children of recent immigrants. During and after World War I many communities felt an intense concern for "Americanization" of children from foreign cultural backgrounds.

The nineteenth century has attracted increasing attention from family historians. Resources for quantitative studies abound, including tax lists, probate court records, and the United States census through 1880. Family letters, diaries, wills, tax lists, city directories, and other materials are also relatively abundant. Much of the research thus far deals with changing birth rates, geographical movement, and the family's function in the process of urbanization and economic change.[10] Other studies discuss the evolving situations of

10 Among the most interesting are Bernard Farber, *Guardians of Virtue: Salem Families in 1800* (New York, 1972); John Modell, "Family and Fertility on the Indiana Frontier, 1820," *American Quarterly* 23 (December 1971), pp. 615-634; Modell and Tamara K. Hareven, "Urbanization and the Malleable Household: An Examination of Boarding and Lodging in American Families," *Journal of Marriage and the Family* 35 (August 1973), pp. 467-479; Robert E. Bieder, "Kinship as a Factor in Migration," *ibid.* pp. 429-439; Richard A. Easterlin, "Factors in the Decline of Farm Family Fertility in the United States: Some Preliminary Research Results," *Journal of American History* 63 (December 1976), pp. 600-614; Stephen Thernstrom, *Poverty and Progress: Social Mobility in a Nineteenth Century City* (Cambridge, Mass., 1964) and *The Other Bostonians: Poverty and Progress in the American Metropolis, 1880-1970* (Cambridge, Mass., 1973); Howard Chudacoff, *Mo-*

women and children.[11] The black family, both before and after the Civil War, attracts much interest.[12]

It has been difficult to study the American family in the twentieth century for various reasons. Many of the materials used to investigate earlier periods are unavailable. Individual federal census returns—the most valuable single source of information on the total population—have not been released. Family records often remain in private hands and frequently do not exist at all. Published studies of the family rely on conventional public records or limited sociological surveys.[13] The scarcity of other resources for studying the institution of the family in recent years makes collections of individual family histories such as yours particularly valuable.

American family historians have thus far exposed only the bare outlines of their subject, but they have offered some interesting and useful insights. The nuclear family—husband, wife, and their natural children—appears to have been the American norm since early colonial days. Other persons have often been present in the household (slaves, servants in the colonial period, boarders in the nineteenth century, and aged grandparents until rather recently), but the extended family—large kinship living units, including several couples and spanning three or four generations—has been rare. Marriage usually involved establishing a separate household rather than living with either set of parents, a practice common in some societies. Among other things, this may help to explain the rapid expan-

bile Americans: Residential and Social Mobility in Omaha, 1880-1920 (New York, 1972); Kirk Jeffrey, "The Family as Utopian Retreat from the City: The Nineteenth Century Contribution," in The Family, Communes, and Utopian Societies, ed. Sallie TeSelle (New York, 1972), pp. 21-41; and Richard Sennett, Families Against the City: Middle Class Homes of Industrial Chicago, 1872-1890 (Cambridge, Mass., 1964). Tamara K. Hareven, ed., Anonymous Americans: Explorations in Nineteenth-Century Social History (Englewood Cliffs, N.J., 1971) is a valuable collection of articles.

11 Barbara Welter, "The Cult of True Womanhood: 1820-1860," American Quarterly 18 (Summer 1966), pp. 151-174; Carroll Smith-Rosenberg, "Beauty, the Beast, and the Militant Woman: A Case Study in Sex Roles and Social Stress in Jacksonian America," ibid. 23 (October 1971), pp. 562-584; David M. Kennedy, "The Nineteenth Century Heritage: The Family, Feminism, and Sex," in Birth Control in America: The Career of Margaret Sanger (New York, 1970), pp. 36-71; Bernard Wishy, The Child and the Republic: The Dawn of Modern American Child-Nurture (Philadelphia, 1968); and Kathryn Kish Sklar, Catherine Beecher: A Study in American Domesticity (New Haven, Conn., 1973).

12 John Blassingame, The Slave Community (New York, 1972); Frank J. Furstenberg, Jr., Theodore Hershberg, and John Modell, "The Origins of the Female-Headed Black Family: The Impact of the Urban Experience," Journal of Interdisciplinary History 6 (Autumn 1975), pp. 211-233; Crandall A. Shifflett, "The Household Composition of Rural Black Families: Louisa County, Virginia, 1880," ibid. pp. 235-260; and Herbert Gutman, The Negro Family in Slavery and Freedom, 1750-1925 (New York, 1976).

13 William L. O'Neill, Divorce in the Progressive Era (New Haven, Conn., 1967), and William H. Chafe, The American Woman: Her Changing Social, Economic, and Political Role, 1920-1970 (New York, 1972), are the most important historical analyses. Several sociological surveys of communities or groups are helpful in coming to terms with the twentieth century American family: Robert and Helen Lynd, Middletown (New York, 1929) and Middletown in Transition (New York, 1937); Franklin Frazier, The Negro Family in the United States (Chicago, 1939); Robert J. Havinghurst and H. Gerthon Morgan, The Social History of a War-Boom Community (New York, 1951); Oscar Lewis, La Vida (New York, 1966); and Glen H. Elder, Children of the Great Depression: Social Change in Life Experience (Chicago, 1974).

sion of settled territory and the high mobility of American families. Frequent disruption of the family unit through early departure of children, premature death of a spouse, or divorce, has been typical in America as has been the tendency of the individual cast adrift to join some new family unit.

Divorce and death provide major disruptions in family life. Their impact on individuals and the remaining family unit merit careful consideration. This student has investigated the reasons for as well as the effect of her grandmother's divorces.

Susan, age 11, was happy to have a father again when her mother married James Tobin, a factory security guard. They started spending time as a family with his relatives. He treated her very nicely. The newlyweds started fighting in a few months, and he left within nine months.

When Susan was twelve years old, Virginia married Ed Stout. Stout worked at the Ford Willow Run Plant. He had two other children, a son who was a captain away in the war, and a daughter who lived in an apartment. Stout was very nice to his new daughter. Susan was a little embarrassed at having a second stepfather and at first didn't mention it to her friends. The couple was only married a little over a year and then divorced. Susan remembers the cause of the divorces being her mother's insistence on living in the same house, running things as she wanted to, and always making more money than her husband because she was working as a cook in fine restaurants and country clubs by this time. Also Virginia had a severe drinking problem.

Virginia's drinking became worse after her divorces. The mother-child relationship was poor; it consisted of beatings and yelling. Susan was ashamed of her mother's behavior, her drinking and having so many boyfriends. Susan was very religious. During a family crisis, she would spend time at a friend's home or church and school social activities which alleviated pressures from home. Close friends' parents realized Susan's home situation and took her on their family activities.

Since the beginning of the nineteenth century, the size of the American family has fallen steadily. In 1800 the average number of children born to a white woman who survived to the end of her childbearing years was just over seven. By 1900 the average had dropped to 3.5. In 1975 it was 1.9. This shift may have both reflected and caused alterations in the nature of the family. The economic functions of the family changed as more and more work moved out of the home and into factories and offices. During the nineteenth and early twentieth centuries, women and children grew less involved in making a family's living, and large families became less necessary for income production and old-age security for parents. Meanwhile, the economic, educational, and emotional burdens of children on their parents, especially mothers, grew greater. In the nineteenth century, childhood became increasingly recognized as a distinct stage of life, one properly devoted to education rather than work to assist the family. Between 1848 and 1918 all states adopted compulsory school attendance laws, reflecting both a growing concern for education and a shift of responsibility in this area from the family to government. Somewhat later, government began to assume responsibility for old-age and unemployment security, thereby absorbing what had formerly been family obligations. As family size and domestic burdens declined, the household role of women was reduced, and the feminist quest for opportunities outside the home expanded. Finally, beginning in World War II, it became common for married women of all ages to work outside the home, giving them a new degree of independence and identity separate from their long-standing family roles as wives and mothers.

Another informative school picture makes a dramatic point of the number of students in relation to the size of this one-room school. Note also the range of ages and the attire of the students.

As America evolved over the past century from a largely rural and small-town nation to a mass, urban, and industrial society with a high degree of mobility, individuals lost a measure of the security which stemmed from understanding their place in a stable community. People apparently came to depend more heavily upon their immediate family for emotional support. The century-long rise in the divorce rate—from one per sixteen marriages in 1890 to one per seven marriages by 1920 and one per four marriages in 1970—and the high rate of remarriage suggests this. "There is no golden age of the family gleaming at us from far back in the historical past. And there is no good reason to construe recent trends in terms of decline and decay," John Demos persuasively argues. "Perhaps we seek more from marriage than did our forebearers—more intimacy, more openness, more deep-down emotional support."14 When a marriage has failed to satisfy their needs, Americans

14 "The American Family in Past Time," *American Scholar* 43 (Summer 1974), p. 444.

have shown a growing willingness to dissolve it and to seek another.

Certainly the history of the American family involves changing functions, recast economic and child nurture responsibilities, and altered patterns of emotional relationships. The details of the changes, even more so their significance, are as yet perceived only dimly. It is difficult to measure and interpret, for example, signs of significant and longterm increases of sexual activity inside and out of marriage. However, reduced parental authority, increased emphasis on romantic love as a basis for marriage, spreading knowledge of contraceptive techniques, and revised moral attitudes all appear to be involved. Also obscure are the nature and causes of variations in family patterns among blacks, ethnics, and old stock whites as well as among families on different economic levels. Nevertheless, it is increasingly clear that as America in general has changed, the family has changed as well.

This photo of girls dressed for a church celebration, the crowning of the Virgin Mary, provides evidence as to the role of religion in one Italian Catholic family.

Historians are learning more about the American family's past so rapidly that any attempt as synthesis is likely to be quickly outdated.[15] Obviously much more needs to be learned, especially about the twentieth century family, before a reliable overview can be developed. A great variety of informational resources—from manuscript collections to census returns, to

15 Demos' short essay, *ibid.*, pp. 422-446, Edward Shorter, *The Making of the Modern Family* (New York, 1975), and Tamara K. Hareven, "Family Time and Historical Time," *Daedalus* (Spring 1977), pp. 57-70, are ambitious and thoughtful efforts at synthesis and general analysis. All are limited, and Shorter's conclusions in particular have been severely criticized by other historians of the family. Three excellent collections of articles reflect the fragmented nature of recent inquiry: Theodore K. Rabb and Robert I. Rotberg, eds., *The Family in History: Interdisciplinary Essays* (New York, 1973); Michael Gordon, ed., *The American Family in Social-Historical Perspective* (New York, 1973), and Tamara K. Hareven, ed., *Family and Kin in Urban Communities, 1700-1930* (New York, 1977).

individual family histories—can all contribute to clarifying a still-cloudy picture.

The health of family members and the medical care that they are able to obtain frequently becomes an important factor in a family's story. A comparison of the manner in which babies were delivered from one generation to next, for instance, may tell much about changing standards of medical practice and the family's attitudes toward such matters. In this excerpt, the author has shown vividly the emotional strain placed on one family by a series of unfortunate births.

In August 1912, Lillian delivered another daughter, named Sara. But the baby was born dead. She was a very large baby and the doctor had to use instruments for the birth. It was a terrible delivery, and by the time the infant was born, she was dead. This birth was the portent of other tragic ones to come. Lillian had exceptionally large babies, and was evidently too narrow in the pelvic area to deliver them. If she had lived a few decades later, her babies would undoubtedly have been delivered by the Cesarean section. But Lillian was a young mother in the early 1900s, and she bore the tragedy of the faulty medical skill of that era.

The following year, on August 30, 1913, Charles and Lillian's first son was born. He was named James Harvey after his maternal grandfather. This baby was also very large, weighing twelve pounds. He lived, however, although much of his young life would cause concern for his parents. James or Jim, was destined to have pneumonia five times and kidney failure when he was eight years old. His life was fortunate to be spared, as he, too, would not be much helped by the doctors' ability at that time, before antibiotic drugs.

Arthur was born in August 1916, but would die in 2½ years from a sudden illness. Clyde arrived in May 1919, but he, too, would die the following September, because of pneumonia. Ruth came in July 1922. The mines nearby had closed, so Charles moved his wife and three children onto a farm where they could live off the land. Another boy, named Jack, was born to Lillian in September 1925. He was huge—15 pounds. The doctor simply could not make a safe delivery, and the baby's neck was broken by using forceps; Jack was stillborn.

After Jack's birth, Lillian's health began to deteriorate. The hard life of a miner's wife, the worry caused by Albert's illnesses, and the hard births that ended in deaths took their toll on her health. She was 35 years old and beginning to have diabetes. Her hair began to whiten, and Lillian just became generally ill for long periods in the following years.

Lillian bore another child, named Ray, on November 30, 1927. She became so ill that Bessie, her oldest daughter, had no other choice than to stay home from high school and take care of the house and her mother. The baby had come through a hard delivery, and had eczema and unknown allergies. Ray cried most of the time, and his hands had to be tied to the buggy sides to prevent his scratching himself. Jim and Bessie walked the baby for hours, trying to help him and their mother. Nothing much really helped. Ray, a beautiful red-haired baby, died when he was 18 months old.

PRESERVING AND SHARING YOUR FAMILY'S HISTORY

One important way to enlarge our understanding of the patterns of American family life is to bring together significant numbers of individual family histories. One way of doing this is for any group or class doing family histories at the same time to discuss and compare their results. A more lasting and far-reaching effect is possible if the histories are gathered together and deposited with a reliable caretaker. A family history collection generated, for instance, by students at a particular high school or college, or by members of a church congregation,

PRESERVING AND SHARING YOUR FAMILY'S HISTORY

Wedding portraits often reveal interesting relationships within families and between friends. This 1921 picture could be used as an opener in an interview with any of the persons in it who are still alive.

could make clearer the institution's past as well as the nature of its constituency. An even larger collection based on one community may allow a researcher to identify broader patterns and to develop useful insights. Such collections do not describe societies with statistical precision, but they do contribute to a fuller understanding of family life in that community.

Students writing family histories often find it painful to look at a family hardship or decline, although these are often as much a part of the story as success and progress. This author obtained several valuable insights by analyzing the reasons for her parents' problems and the ways in which other family members aided them.

Virginia married young, and had so many children so often, that she soon found herself in a much different lifestyle than her parents had experienced. Ralph always had mining work, but they stayed poor. He drank too much and caused many problems within the home. Virginia's own life had been cushioned (and her father had rarely drunk alcohol), so that she now faced problems that she could not handle. Samuel and Jane helped their daughter as much as possible. All the produce and milk the young family needed was from their farm. Much of the meat they butchered was sent to Virginia and Ralph. One winter Jane even sent butter through the mail to her daughter; it would not melt in the cold weather, and was gratefully received. So Ralph and Virginia's children never went hungry, but most of the comforts of life were missing.

There are several ways to preserve family histories for the benefit of your family, the community, and researchers. The first, but most limited in effect, is to make sure a copy is placed with other valuable family records wherever they are kept. A better solution would be to find an institution which would be prepared to give permanent storage and care to family histories. The national Anonymous Families History Project accepts student papers done according to its guidelines (available upon request from Professor Tamara K. Hareven, Department of History, Clark University, Worcester, Mass. 01610). Some regional archives—the University of Akron American History Research Center and the Louisiana State University Department of Archives and Manuscripts, to name but two—have received family histories from the area they serve. Perhaps your state or local historical society, your public library, or a nearby university has such a collection or would be willing to start one if asked. In many cases, an instructor supervising family history projects in connection with a course will have made arrangements already for their deposit and will notify you. If not, ask.

This account of homesteading on the Great Plains not only describes a common nineteenth century American family experience, but also shows what one student was able to learn about her grandparents from various official records.

Ole and Karie settled in the Sheyenne River Valley in Griggs County, Dakota Territory. The area was still sparsely settled, having only been opened by Norwegians from Iowa in a covered wagon drawn by two oxen. The area they settled included land along the river, green with shade trees and cool on hot summer days, and acreage on the fertile prairie up form the riverbanks. Their first home was dugout on a hillside where they lived for two years. Ole, in the meantime, cut trees near the river and made a log house with a shingle roof. This was known as the "palace of the prairie" for many years.

Under the Homestead Act, a settler could obtain land free by remaining on a claim for five years and improving it, or he could pay a prescribed sum of money for the same acreage and reduce the time of residence necessary for ownership. After living on and improving the land for nearly three years, Ole took out the Pre-Emption Proof papers on the 160 acres he had settled. He paid $2.50 an acre for it, and the papers show that he took up residence on the land on July 10, 1880, and that his first act was to build a dwelling. By the date of the certificate, June 30, 1883, he, his wife and two daughters were living there, and he had broken 32 acres and had raised 215 bushels of wheat and 160 bushels of oats.

To fulfill the requirements of the Homestead Act, three neighbors attested to the time of residence, the improvements, the amount of fencing, and what crops were raised. John Torfin, Andrew Torfin and Omund Nelson, the first white settlers in the entire area, all spoke as witnesses for Ole. They each verified the existence of the "dwelling house, log, two log stables, one straw shed, well, 160 rods of rail fence and 32 acres broken."

As a foreigner, Ole could not own land without complying with another requirement of the Homestead Act: "In case the party is of foreign birth, a copy of his declaration of intention to become a citizen or full naturalization certificate, officially certified must be filed with the case." This he had filed originally in Iowa, but followed up with the "Declaration Register" in August, 1883. His full citizenship was granted in the name of Ole Johnson Skrien on June 18, 1889. The 160 acres on the Sheyenne River in Dakota Territory were his on July 3, 1883.

If a repository for your family history either exists or can be started, you should consider carefully whether or not to contribute to it. Is the institution doing the collecting committed to

The background of this picture gives clues to the economic status and taste of the couple photographed.

preserving the family histories permanently? Will adequate care and storage be provided so that they will neither be damaged nor lost? Furthermore, is the institution willing to publicize the existence of its family history collection? If deposited at this institution, would your history be accessible to family members? Will members of the family resent your deposit? Is the institution prepared to respect and defend your family's right of privacy?

A family history collection can be a very valuable resource, provided it is carefully preserved and not abandoned after a few years. It may be consulted by researchers and contribute to a fuller appreciation of the American past or a better understanding of society's current needs. Generally, those institutions, such as libraries and archives, with long experience and commitment to caring for and making available written records, are the most reliable custodians. Deposited where it will be protected and used along with other documents, your family history becomes a part of *recorded* American history. Your family's activities and achievements, trials and tribulations, will not be overlooked by those seeking to understand the American family, nor will that information be lost to your own descendants.

Your decision to deposit your family history should not rest solely upon the availability of a dependable institution which will care for it and will make it available to researchers. You and your family have rights and interests which should be respected. You and others mentioned in your family history understandably may not wish to be identified in the publications or statements of unknown researchers who read your account. Family members who are quite willing to share intimate details with you may consider general exposure of such matters to be an invasion of their privacy. Do not commit yourself to deposit just because an instructor who will be grading your paper is someone you like and admire and recommends that you do it, unless your interests are protected and your family agrees. Any responsible institution will recognize and defend your legitimate rights of privacy and will do its best to see that researchers do likewise. Researchers using a family history collection generally are interested in broad patterns and trends rather than in individual cases; therefore they neither need nor care to use individual names. It is reasonable and appropriate to ask the institution receiving your family history to forbid anyone from publishing or otherwise publicly repeat-

---

Religion plays an important part in the lives of some families. This student's description of religious practices and attitudes helped him to explain how his grandmother coped with discrimination and poverty.

After a long and hard week, Sundays rolled around and people took their religion seriously; it was the only hope a Black person had. It let the people let out all of their frustrations, angry contempt, and hopelessness. For one day it brought the Black people together in their Sunday best, ready to bow their heads to the Lord and ask the Lord for strength to face the coming cold, cruel, hard week. Religion made the people happy, it gave the people strength to endure and survive.

So everyone gathered underneath one roof and the pastor preached from his heart and the services were long and beautiful. The church generally rocked with spirit and the soul of Black people. After church everyone said their formal goodbyes and got ready to go and enjoy a good Sunday dinner and relax and enjoy this one glorious day, but never pushing the oncoming week out of their minds.

By now Grandmother had settled down in the system, she had a place in the system and she hated her status. She had to go in the backdoor of stores, restaurants, and sit in the back of the bus but she still held her head up high.

Grandmother said that she was born Black and that was the way it was meant to be. She was proud to be Black, always had been and always will be proud, she always stated. She gave her children these values about being Black and proud and always holding your head up high. She also said, "Know yourself and who you are in all your Blackness and it will give you the strength to be a strong person."

The South in which Grandmother had lived all her life didn't have anything more to offer her. So she migrated North in search of a dream in which she wasn't issued second-class citizenship, where she could get a good job so that her children could have a better job, a better education, and a better life than she had.

ing names of living persons obtained from the family history without your permission and, if you wish, the permission of other individuals involved. This will not interfere with legitimate research, and it will protect your interests.

If you decide to give your family history to a library, an archives, or other institution collecting such materials, you should include a signed statement describing the terms of the donation and the rights and obligations of the institution receiving it. A satisfactory form for this purpose can be found on page 00 of this handbook. This is a standard and very important procedure. Acceptance of your paper with this statement attached acknowledges the institution's willingness to abide by the specified terms. You can assist the repository in administering its family history collection and in directing researchers only to those papers they need to see by including the checklist index on page 71.

The date and location of a photograph can sometimes be determined from the picture itself, though seldom as easily as in this camping scene.

After you have resolved the question of what to do with your completed family history, you are finally finished. Your curiosity, of course, may cause you to continue doing research and eventually lead you to write a revised or expanded version of your family history. But even if you never do another thing with your project you have truly acted as an historian. You have sought to understand the complex elements which make up the past and the process of change over time. You have carried out the same activities that a professional historian engages in: gathering information from a variety of written, oral, pictorial, and possibly other sources; assessing its reliability; organizing your data; analyzing and interpreting their meaning; coping with gaps in the record; writing your conclusions; and making your results available to others. From among the infinite number of surviving fragments of information about the past, you have identified and made sense of some which help to explain your own background and current situation. You can take well-deserved satisfaction in your accomplishment. You have added to your own, and perhaps others' understanding of your family's and America's past.

Both commonplace and unusual aspects of family life may be reflected in old letters. Although letters often are discarded, many families tend to save ones to and from members away on a trip or military duty. The questions asked as well as the information contained in such letters can provide insights. For instance, in this 1864 letter to her husband who was away fighting in the Civil War, a wife revealed quite a bit about the family's economic situation and the relationship between man and wife.

Perhaps you would like to know what we are going to have for dinner. I am going to have a piece of sow belly and greens and mashed potatoes and stewed rhubarb and a cup of tea and bread and butter and how well I would enjoy it if you was here to help eat it . . .

Well, dear Will, I am now up at Lew and Harriett's . . . and I thought I would finish writing my letter for I have got some good ink which I did not have at home . . . .

I went in to the store last Thursday and I got Sam a suit of clothes and Leroy a pair of shoes and pants and Esther a dress and two pair of pants and a pair of shoes. When I came home I was minus $11 and 25 cents and that is all I got. I looked for hats for the boys and for Esther, but I found my money would not hold out and I had to come home without them. I do not know how I can get along without a pair of shoes for myself and a dress of some kind and a hat.

I wish that Pringle would pay over, which he seems no way inclined to do. I do not know the man and as there is more of the same kind of name in town you ought to have told me his name, gave me written order or something to show that I had authority to collect it. I thought I would get the things I mentioned on trust, but I have been into the stores with the girls two or three times and the store keepers are so afraid I will ask for trust they will hardly turn round to show me their goods. And if I ask the price they will just tell me and never pretend to show them to me. I went down to the sew store and I bought 8 yards of calico and I handed Nusbaum a $5.00 bill. Then he was all attention and fell considerably on his goods. So by their actions I have come to the conclusion if can't have the money I will grease and go naked before I will ask for trust.

FURTHER READING

In a rapidly evolving field of study, it is more useful to indicate those journals in which the latest findings regularly appear than to dwell too extensively on older works. A number of outstanding articles and books have been identified already

Interviews can provide details which otherwise might be lost about events large and small. In this interview, the small details of one generation's wedding customs were recalled, and a great deal is revealed about the family's relationship to the community in which they lived.

Usually a relative of the couple, a young man, was asked to ride through the country on horseback, selecting the families he was to invite. They in turn would pin a ribbon on the rider's hat or tie it on the horse's bridle if they'd accept. This was done a week or more before the wedding. A couple days before the wedding the neighbors would help set up. The women would clean the house and the men would clean the haymow for the dance if it was warm enough. They'd clean up the yard, too.

The day before the wedding the younger ladies would bake oodles of pies and cookies and cakes. Cakes and cookies were baked earlier sometimes, but having no refrigerators the pies had to wait until the day before. The older ladies would peel a couple bushels of potatoes. They would put them in large milk cans and then put real cold water on them and keep them in the cellar overnight.

The ceremony would be at 10:30 a.m. and as soon as the couple came home they'd start serving. Some weddings they'd serve three tables at a time. Always two, at least. Dishes and cooking utensils were borrowed from neighbors. Some would rent dishes. Two full meals were served, but later years the ceremony was usually at 2:00 p.m., with only one full meal. Lunch was served late evening. Cookies several times a day. Craziest custom was the chivaree, when a group would come to serenade the couple.

in footnotes. Although they focus on a wider range of topics, the *American Quarterly, Journal of Social History*, and *Journal of Interdisciplinary History* have paid considerable attention to American family history. Concentrating even more closely on the subject are the *Journal of Marriage and the Family*, the *Journal of Psychohistory* (formerly the *History of Childhood Quarterly*), and the new *Journal of Family History*.

For additional advice on writing an individual family history, see David H. Culbert, "Undergraduates as Historians: Family History Projects Add Meaning to an Introductory Survey," *History Teacher* 7 (November 1973), pp. 7-17; Kirk Jeffrey, "Write a History of Your Own Family: Further Observations and Suggestions for Instructors," *ibid.* (May 1974), pp. 365-373; and Jim Watts and Allen F. Davis, *Generations: Your Family in Modern American History* (New York, 1974). Three articles in the *American Archivist* 38 (October 1975) discuss collections of individual family histories and their relationship to broader studies: David E. Kyvig, "Family History: New Opportunities for Archivists," pp. 509-519; Kirk Jeffrey, "Varieties of Family History," pp. 521-532; and David H. Culbert, "Family History Projects: The Scholarly Value of the Informal Sample," pp. 533-541.

Helpful examples of different approaches to collecting information on individuals and their families through oral interviewing are Dorothy Gallagher, *Hannah's Daughters: Six Generations of an American Family, 1876-1976* (New York, 1976); Kathy Kahn, *Hillbilly Women* (New York, 1972); Studs Terkel, *Working* (New York, 1972); James Agee and Walker Evans, *Let*

Us Now Praise Famous Men (New York, 1941); Theodore Rosengarten, *All God's Dangers: The Life of Nate Shaw* (New York, 1974); and *These Are Our Lives (as told by the people and written by members of the Federal Writers' Project of the Works Progress Administration in North Carolina, Tennessee, and Georgia)* (Chapel Hill, N.C., 1939)

Finding this photo in a family album suggested to the researcher that her grandfather did at least some of the family's butchering.

David Weitzman, *Underfoot: An Everyday Guide to Exploring the American Past* (New York, 1976), provides insight into material culture. Among other subjects, Weitzman deals with copying and preserving photographs, reading tombstones, interpreting cemetery symbols, and digging historical information out of old mills, abandoned machinery, unearthed bottles, and historical buildings. Also valuable is Robert A. Weinstein and Larry Booth, *The Collection, Use, and Care of Historical Photographs* (Nashville: American Association for State and Local History, 1976).

Persons interested in genealogical research will find these to be useful guides: Gilbert Doane, *Searching for Your Ancestors* (4th ed., New York, 1974); George B. Everton, *Handybook for Genealogists* (Logan, Utah, 1971); Val Greenwood, *The Researcher's Guide to American Genealogy* (New York, 1974); Jeane Eddy Westin, *Finding Your Roots* (Los Angeles, 1977); and Ethel W. Williams, *Know Your Ancestors: A Guide to Genealogical Research* (Rutland, Vt., 1960). The monthly *Journal of Genealogy* and *The Genealogical Helper*, published bimonthly by the Everton Publishers (P.O. Box 368, Logan, Utah 84321), are helpful periodicals.

The popularity of Alex Haley's *Roots* and the television series based on it has inspired considerable interest in genealogy among American blacks. Charles L. Blockson, *Black Genealogy*

(Englewood Cliffs, N. J., 1977) is a very useful guide for historians as well as genealogists. Of similar interest is Dan Rottenberg, *Finding our Fathers: A Guidebook to Jewish Genealogy* (New York, 1977).

Persons interested in investigating family or geographical names should consult *Names: Journal of the American Name Society*, published quarterly since 1951.

Some families keep records of their major purchases and everyday expenses which help in an understanding of their lives. A receipt for a new automobile and an account book show what it cost to buy and maintain a car in 1930. Another page in the account book indicates that the owner's income for the year was $1200.

Mining has always been difficult work, although like other jobs, it has changed over the years. As in other industries, labor unions often had an influence on working conditions. This student carefully described her grandfather's job, the efforts of the United Mine Workers to organize the mine in which he worked, and his feelings about all this.

Going into and out of the mines took a long time. Although the miners only worked 8 hours the trips to their rooms usually added an extra half-hour each way. In one mine Jim traveled on the cars for 1 hour and 15 minutes to and from the working area. That was two-and-one-half hours extra to his actual working time.

The men needed a union to help with their rights. United Mine Workers' organizers came to Yatesboro in the summer of 1930 to set up a union. But the company hired (and the state paid for) the Coal and Iron Police to come into town and chase out the organizers. Billy clubs and guns were carried by the mounted police, and they effectively dispersed the U.M.W. men.

After Franklin Roosevelt was elected in 1932, the U.M.W. was allowed to operate in Yatesboro. The theater building was used for a union hall, and the men were simply told to sign up. It was so different from the first unsuccessful attempt to unionize. After the U.M.W. came in, the men were undoubtedly less at the mercy of the company. Wages were set, and a check weighman was allowed to join the company weighman who gave the decisions concerning how much each miner had worked. Before the union the company's man could cheat the men of the number of cars they had filled. After the union, the U.M.W. check weighman was there to insure that the miners were credited their full amount.

John L. Lewis was the idol of the miners. He obviously had helped the men, and was greatly respected. Around May, 1934, John L. (as he was affectionately called) held a rally in Indiana. James and Linda Bowers took John Peters and went to hear the huge leader speak. Of course, all of the miners were grateful to him; but James thought there was nobody to equal him. And perhaps he was right, because John L. did accomplish many things for the men underground. Although John felt that John L. later took too much power into his own hands, he could never deny that the U.M.W. leader had always looked after the workers.

Pictures in a family album often relate to events which the family considered important. Buying their first car, a used Model "A" roadster, filled this soon-to-be-married young couple with pride.

Immigrant groups brought various cultural traditions to America. Inquiring about such practices, learning what was retained, modified, and abandoned as well as the point at which this happened can indicate the ways in which a family adjusted to life in a new location.

Though the immigrants brought few belongings from Norway, they carried many traditions with them. They had special foods on religious holidays, even though they were far away from home. At Christmas, they did their best to have lutefisk and lefse, the mainstay of the holiday fare in Norway. Sweet desserts, many made with cream, were a tasty end to the meal. The Christmas cookies were often fried, one at a time, and either rolled out thinly and deep-fat fried as in the case of fattigmon, or perhaps dipped in batter and fried on a iron in deep fat as with rosettes. Krumkaka batter was placed in an iron and heated over the fire, then formed into cones and filled. One consistent food was rommegrot, or cream mush, a mixture made of cream, boiled with flour until the butter ran off, then served with cinnamon, sugar and the butter.

Typical of the holiday gifts in the pioneer home were perhaps a knife for the boys and a doll head for the girls. Oranges were a special treat highly valued by the children. Toys in those days were homemade, simple and allowed for much imagination. A "bicycle" was simply a wheel with a stick through the middle held in both hands by the "operator" who then ran behind it as fast as he could and with luck would win the "bicycle race."

Stick games played with a group of children were always fun. Prakaball was played with at least four or more people, a ball and a stick. Each person had a hole in front of him, and kept his stick in it, if he could. One person was "it" in the center and tried to get his stick and the ball into another's base by striking the other sticks, or otherwise coaxing them to take the stick out of the hole.

This woman's pride in her garden is obvious in this snapshot.

Family hardship has taken many forms, and the discovery of the reasons behind it sometimes requires considerable probing. Here are descriptions of two important varieties of hardship—social discrimination and economic difficulty—and their impact on one family.

In the twenties the Ku Klux Klan began to march through the Greek community at night and spread terror through their demonstrations. The children were frightened by the frequent cross burnings, and also suffered taunts from their classmates at school. Ann recalls how she lost her best friend when her playmate's parents realized that Ann was "a Greek." And on one hot autumn night, the Ku Klux Klan burned down the farm of one Greek, who then moved his family to Chicago.

Early in 1929, an Atlantic and Pacific (A. & P.) chain market opened two blocks from the family's grocery store. Many of the customers who frequented Gregory's now took their business to the more inexpensive market down the street. After October of 1929, business went farther downhill. Bills could no longer be paid off. By 1930, Gregory was forced to sell his home and grocery store in order to feed and clothe his family.

G. W. HANSON

Superintendent of Public Sch____

FOR

IRON COUNTY, MISSOURI

Office Day—SATURDAY
PHONE 108

Ironton, Mo.
March 15th, 1921

Dear Student :-

      You have passed the final examination on the work for this year ### and will be classed as A-2 next year. You should have no trouble in graduating if you will sepnd the next year in school and work hard. I trust that you will go to school every day and make good grades and after you finish the 8th grade, I hope you will be able to go to high school somewhere. The time has come when every boy and girl needs a high school education and I believe you are going to get one. It will mean so much to you in the future. Don't let anything keep you from striving onward and upward. The world is before you and we want you to take advantage of the opportunities which are yours.

      We do not send the grades but you had to make an average grade of 80% to pass. You will know your grades at the beginning of the term next year.

      Trusting that you will go ahead with your work, I am,

                      Very truly yours,

                      G. W. Hanson, Co. Supt. Schools.

School diplomas are valuable documents, though few are as informal and informative as this.

Leisure time activities may, if shared, draw a family together or, if pursued independently, lead an individual away from the family group. Thus it is important to consider what family members do with their leisure time. Technology has significantly altered use of leisure as well as other facets of life. The impact of the automobile on the family's life style is worth considering. In this excerpt, a student discusses how another important technology, television, affected his family. Note how each generation reacted differently.

Our first TV set was purchased in 1956 when I was approximately one year old. This highly significant occurrence was no mere accident nor was it a lightly-considered decision. Even by that time, when TV was in its infancy, Mom had become a devotee. She recalled for me her first impression of TV: She and my father-to-be had occasion, on one of their dates, to be in a local establishment which boasted one of the first TVs in the area. For the enjoyment of patrons, of course, and possibly to attract a few customers, the TV was on. Mom stared at the TV in fascination and exclaimed, "Sam can you believe that's happening RIGHT NOW!" Shortly before my birth my family moved adjacent to my maternal grandparents, who were among the first in town to own a television. Then, according to Mom, we would often gather at my grandparents' house to watch. Thus influenced, and for the good of the four children, aged one to three, who would soon be old enough to appreciate it, Mom told Dad that we simply had to have a TV.

For good or bad, then, my brothers, sister, and I have grown up with television. Much of our leisure time as children and adolescents was squandered in front of the "boob tube." There often was bitter competition for a chair since none of us cared to sit on the floor. Such childhood dedication to TV doubtless many times rescued my mother from the dilemma of keeping four small children occupied.

I was a devotee of the Saturday cartoons, Bugs Bunny, Daffy Duck, Mickey Mouse, Quick Draw McGraw, Huckleberry Hound, and others. The Three Stooges was my favorite Sunday morning program. It aired from 7 – 9 in the morning, and I recall watching it in its entirety many a Sunday morn before I went to mass. The single most impressive moment that I recall, of all my TV viewing experiences as a small child, occurred one Sunday afternoon as I watched, with my father, a dramatic conflict between a haggard band of U.S. soldiers and the entire German army. The impressive moment, which will live forever in my memory, ensued as Hitler addressed a huge gathering of impeccably arrayed German soldiers. I was fearful until my father explained my worries away. No single program has come close to recreating as eerie a feeling or as thrilling a moment as that brief film strip of Hitler.

The assassination of John F. Kennedy occurred when I was eight. Excessive exposure to the TV coverage of his funeral and its many attendant substories left me seriously depressed and withdrawn for several days. The assassination of Robert Kennedy 4½ years later had a similar impact. Any lasting effects of these two events on me, I am certain, can be attributed in no small way to the vividness of TV. I remember distinctly the stark procession of JFK's funeral cortege on our old black-and-white RCA.

As we children became increasingly fond of TV, our parents wielded its privileges to compel our compliance or obedience. "You can't watch TV until . . ." was a familiar phrase. Many a Saturday morning (when I was between eight and eleven) my brothers and I would be guiltily watching TV when our angry father would walk down the hall to the den, turn the TV off, and tell us to go to work in the yard. When I was thirteen or fourteen my parents jointly issued a "no-TV-after-eight-on-school-nights" decree. This was precipitated by an annoying habit of several members (myself included) to fall asleep in front of the TV (while it was on, of course). This habit, though not excessive, occurred frequently enough to irk my father who sometimes came in late from his office (which was and still is in the back yard) only to find half his family asleep while the TV screamed its staticky message (the day's programming having ended by then). Also, my parents feared that TV was having a detrimental effect on our grades.

Mom and Dad could see the potential dangers of TV and the effects it may have on small children. They liked TV. While for the children it was a major activity, for Mom and Dad it was a source of entertainment and information. My mother has always been a news enthusiast and a lover of science fiction shows and "scary" movies. My father, meanwhile, has always enjoyed sports programs. My family still enjoys TV but it has become less a part of our lives.

This photograph documents Kansas farm life in the 1930s in a way which makes it an invaluable research tool.

Work on a farm was very different from factory work, often demanding the cooperative effort of the entire family. Farm work, too, involved complex procedures. The reminiscences of an eighty year old woman provide details of her experiences with farm work.

Nearly everyone had an orchard and wagonloads of apples in the fall. Cider? Yes, by the barrel. We sorted and put the best apples in the cellar for winter and the rest were ground (one hand-turned mill) into cider. Cider is very sweet and good when fresh, but warm weather turns it hard (intoxicating). I once served cider that was getting hard to a class party unknowingly. I never lived *that* down. The apples which were down each day had to be picked up, peeled and dried. I certainly am not hankering for a return to drying apples. We peeled them and sliced them razor thin. Then we climbed a ladder and spread them out on sheets away from flies. We also covered them with mosquito net. We took them down each night and back up each day until they were dry. We made several sacks of them for apple pie. It was more than we needed but we could not waste because mother always said, "A willful waste will make a woeful want."

The authors.

David E. Kyvig

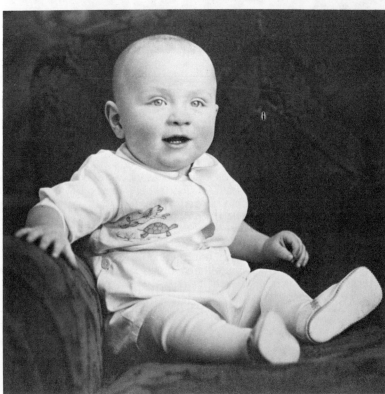

Myron A. Marty

Family History Deposit Agreement

I hereby donate this family history, entitled _____

_____

and dated _____, along with all literary and administrative

rights thereto, to _____.

In accepting this family history, the above named institution obtains the right to make the document available for use by all researchers whom it deems qualified, provided the researcher agrees that no names or other personal characteristics obtained from the document which would identify living persons discussed therein are published or otherwise publicly uttered without my permission and, if I so stipulate at the time of the request, the permission of any person so identified.

Signed _____

Dated _____

Family History Index

1. Your name _____ Sex _____ Age _____ Date _____

2. Check the earliest date for which you have been able to say things about your family in your paper.

   ☐ Before 1750 ☐ 1750-1800 ☐ 1800-1850 ☐ 1850-1900 ☐ 1900 or later

3. Please check *all* regions of the United States in which members of your family whom you have discussed in your paper have lived.

   ☐ New England ☐ Middle Atlantic (NY, PA, NJ, DE, WV, VA, MD) ☐ South Atlantic (GA, FL, NC, SC) ☐ East South Central (LA, MS, AL, TN, KY) ☐ West South Central (AR, AS, NM, TX, OK) ☐ East North Central (MI, IL, OH, WI, IN) ☐ Pacific (CA, OR, WA) ☐ West North Central (MN, IA, SD, ND, NB, KS, MO) ☐ Mountain (MT, WY, CO, UT) ☐ Hawaii, Alaska

4. Please check *all* occupational categories in which members of your family whom you have discussed in this paper have found themselves.

   ☐ Farming ☐ Mining ☐ Shopkeeping or Small Business
   ☐ Transportation ☐ Industrial-Clerical
   ☐ Professions ☐ Industrial-Labor ☐ Military
   ☐ Education ☐ Industrial-Management ☐ Other _____

5. Please check *all* religious groups to which members of your family whom you have discussed in this paper have belonged.

   ☐ Baptist ☐ Lutheran ☐ Quaker
   ☐ Congregational ☐ Methodist ☐ Roman Catholic
   ☐ Episcopalian ☐ Mormon ☐ Other _____
   ☐ Jewish ☐ Presbyterian _____

6. What ethnic or nationality groups are discussed in your paper?

   ☐ African ☐ Filipino ☐ Norwegian
   ☐ Albanian ☐ Finnish ☐ Polish
   ☐ American Indian ☐ French ☐ Puerto Rican
   ☐ Arabic ☐ German ☐ Romanian
   ☐ Armenian ☐ Greek ☐ Russian
   ☐ Austrian ☐ Hungarian ☐ Scottish
   ☐ Black American ☐ Indian ☐ Serbian
   ☐ British ☐ Irish ☐ Slovak
   ☐ Canadian ☐ Italian ☐ Slovenian
   ☐ Chinese ☐ Japanese ☐ Spanish
   ☐ Colombian ☐ Jewish ☐ Swedish
   ☐ Croatian ☐ Korean ☐ Swiss
   ☐ Cuban ☐ Latin American ☐ Ukranian
   ☐ Czech ☐ Lebanese-Syrian ☐ West Indian
   ☐ Danish ☐ Lithuanian ☐ Yugoslav
   ☐ Dutch ☐ Macedonian ☐ Other _____
   ☐ Estonian ☐ Mexican _____

7. What political affiliations of family members are discussed?

   ☐ Democratic ☐ Republican ☐ Other _____

8. What sources did you use in compiling your family history?

   ☐ Interviews with other family members ☐ Land Records
   ☐ Vital Records ☐ Maps
   ☐ Photographs ☐ Family Genealogies
   ☐ Family Bibles ☐ U.S. Census
   ☐ Letters ☐ Other _____
   ☐ Diaries _____

Summary Data Sheet

Writer		Place and Date of Birth	
Place and Date of Marriage			

Names and Birthdates of Children of This Marriage			

Spouse, Place, and Date of Previous or Subsequent Marriage	

Children of Previous or Subsequent Marriage			

Education	Dates	Place	School
Grade School			
High School			
College			
Vocational			

Military Service Dates, Rank, Locations, or Living Arrangements While Spouse in Military	

Employment (Dates)	Occupation	Place	Employer

Religious Affiliation		Fraternal Affiliations	
Political Affiliation		Union Membership	

Organization Membership	
Racial, Ethnic, or Nationality Identification	

Principal Residence Locations Before Marriage (Include Dates)		
Principal Residence Locations After Marriage (Include Dates)		

Summary Data Sheet

Father		Date & Place of Birth	
		Date & Place of Death	

Place and Date of Marriage	

Names and Birthdates of Children of This Marriage			

Spouse, Place, and Date of Previous or Subsequent Marriage	

Children of Previous or Subsequent Marriage		

Education	Dates	Place	School
Grade School			
High School			
College			
Vocational			

Military Service Dates, Rank, Locations, or Living Arrangements While Spouse in Military	

Employment (Dates)	Occupation	Place	Employer

Religious Affiliation		Fraternal Affiliations	
Political Affiliation		Union Membership	

Organization Membership	

Racial, Ethnic, or Nationality Identification	

Principal Residence Locations Before Marriage (Include Dates)		

Principal Residence Locations After Marriage (Include Dates)		

Summary Data Sheet

Mother		Date & Place of Birth	
		Date & Place of Death	

Place and Date of Marriage			

Names and Birthdates of Children of This Marriage			

Spouse, Place, and Date of Previous or Subsequent Marriage	

Children of Previous or Subsequent Marriage			

Education	Dates	Place	School
Grade School			
High School			
College			
Vocational			

Military Service Dates, Rank, Locations, or Living Arrangements While Spouse in Military	

Employment (Dates)	Occupation	Place	Employer

Religious Affiliation		Fraternal Affiliations	
Political Affiliation		Union Membership	

Organization Membership	

Racial, Ethnic, or Nationality Identification	

Principal Residence Locations Before Marriage (Include Dates)		

Principal Residence Locations After Marriage (Include Dates)		

Summary Data Sheet

Maternal Grandmother		Date & Place of Birth	
		Date & Place of Death	
Place and Date of Marriage			
Names and Birthdates of Children of This Marriage			
Spouse, Place, and Date of Previous or Subsequent Marriage			
Children of Previous or Subsequent Marriage			

Education	Dates	Place	School
Grade School			
High School			
College			
Vocational			

Military Service Dates, Rank, Locations, or Living Arrangements While Spouse in Military	

Employment (Dates)	Occupation	Place	Employer

Religious Affiliation		Fraternal Affiliations	
Political Affiliation		Union Membership	
Organization Membership			
Racial, Ethnic, or Nationality Identification			
Principal Residence Locations Before Marriage (Include Dates)			
Principal Residence Locations After Marriage (Include Dates)			

Summary Data Sheet

Maternal Grandfather		Date & Place of Birth	
		Date & Place of Death	

Place and Date of Marriage	

Names and Birthdates of Children of This Marriage			

Spouse, Place, and Date of Previous or Subsequent Marriage	

Children of Previous or Subsequent Marriage			

Education	Dates	Place	School
Grade School			
High School			
College			
Vocational			

Military Service Dates, Rank, Locations, or Living Arrangements While Spouse in Military	

Employment (Dates)	Occupation	Place	Employer

Religious Affiliation		Fraternal Affiliations	
Political Affiliation		Union Membership	

Organization Membership	

Racial, Ethnic, or Nationality Identification	

Principal Residence Locations Before Marriage (Include Dates)		

Principal Residence Locations After Marriage (Include Dates)		

Summary Data Sheet

Paternal Grandmother		Date & Place of Birth	
		Date & Place of Death	

Place and Date of Marriage	

Names and Birthdates of Children of This Marriage			

Spouse, Place, and Date of Previous or Subsequent Marriage	

Children of Previous or Subsequent Marriage			

Education	Dates	Place	School
Grade School			
High School			
College			
Vocational			

Military Service Dates, Rank, Locations, or Living Arrangements While Spouse in Military	

Employment (Dates)	Occupation	Place	Employer

Religious Affiliation		Fraternal Affiliations	
Political Affiliation		Union Membership	

Organization Membership	

Racial, Ethnic, or Nationality Identification	

Principal Residence Locations Before Marriage (Include Dates)		

Principal Residence Locations After Marriage (Include Dates)		

Summary Data Sheet

Paternal Grandfather		Date & Place of Birth	
		Date & Place of Death	
Place and Date of Marriage			
Names and Birthdates of Children of This Marriage			
Spouse, Place, and Date of Previous or Subsequent Marriage			
Children of Previous or Subsequent Marriage			

Education	Dates	Place	School
Grade School			
High School			
College			
Vocational			

Military Service Dates, Rank, Locations, or Living Arrangements While Spouse in Military	

Employment (Dates)	Occupation	Place	Employer

Religious Affiliation		Fraternal Affiliations	
Political Affiliation		Union Membership	
Organization Membership			
Racial, Ethnic, or Nationality Identification			
Principal Residence Locations Before Marriage (Include Dates)			
Principal Residence Locations After Marriage (Include Dates)			

Summary Data Sheet

		Date & Place of Birth	
		Date & Place of Death	
Place and Date of Marriage			
Names and Birthdates of Children of This Marriage			
Spouse, Place, and Date of Previous or Subsequent Marriage			
Children of Previous or Subsequent Marriage			

Education	Dates	Place	School
Grade School			
High School			
College			
Vocational			

Military Service Dates, Rank, Locations, or Living Arrangements While Spouse in Military	

Employment (Dates)	Occupation	Place	Employer

Religious Affiliation		Fraternal Affiliations	
Political Affiliation		Union Membership	

Organization Membership	
Racial, Ethnic, or Nationality Identification	
Principal Residence Locations Before Marriage (Include Dates)	
Principal Residence Locations After Marriage (Include Dates)	

Summary Data Sheet

		Date & Place of Birth	
		Date & Place of Death	
Place and Date of Marriage			
Names and Birthdates of Children of This Marriage			
Spouse, Place, and Date of Previous or Subsequent Marriage			
Children of Previous or Subsequent Marriage			

Education	Dates	Place	School
Grade School			
High School			
College			
Vocational			

Military Service Dates, Rank, Locations, or Living Arrangements While Spouse in Military			

Employment (Dates)	Occupation	Place	Employer

Religious Affiliation		Fraternal Affiliations	
Political Affiliation		Union Membership	
Organization Membership			
Racial, Ethnic, or Nationality Identification			
Principal Residence Locations Before Marriage (Include Dates)			
Principal Residence Locations After Marriage (Include Dates)			

Summary Data Sheet

		Date & Place of Birth	
		Date & Place of Death	
Place and Date of Marriage			
Names and Birthdates of Children of This Marriage			
Spouse, Place, and Date of Previous or Subsequent Marriage			
Children of Previous or Subsequent Marriage			

Education	Dates	Place	School
Grade School			
High School			
College			
Vocational			

Military Service Dates, Rank, Locations, or Living Arrangements While Spouse in Military	

Employment (Dates)	Occupation	Place	Employer

Religious Affiliation		Fraternal Affiliations	
Political Affiliation		Union Membership	

Organization Membership	
Racial, Ethnic, or Nationality Identification	

Principal Residence Locations Before Marriage (Include Dates)		
Principal Residence Locations After Marriage (Include Dates)		

Summary Data Sheet

		Date & Place of Birth	
		Date & Place of Death	
Place and Date of Marriage			
Names and Birthdates of Children of This Marriage			
Spouse, Place, and Date of Previous or Subsequent Marriage			
Children of Previous or Subsequent Marriage			

Education	Dates	Place	School
Grade School			
High School			
College			
Vocational			

Military Service Dates, Rank, Locations, or Living Arrangements While Spouse in Military	

Employment (Dates)	Occupation	Place	Employer

Religious Affiliation		Fraternal Affiliations	
Political Affiliation		Union Membership	

Organization Membership	
Racial, Ethnic, or Nationality Identification	
Principal Residence Locations Before Marriage (Include Dates)	
Principal Residence Locations After Marriage (Include Dates)	

Summary Data Sheet

		Date & Place of Birth	
		Date & Place of Death	
Place and Date of Marriage			
Names and Birthdates of Children of This Marriage			
Spouse, Place, and Date of Previous or Subsequent Marriage			
Children of Previous or Subsequent Marriage			

Education	Dates	Place	School
Grade School			
High School			
College			
Vocational			

Military Service Dates, Rank, Locations, or Living Arrangements While Spouse in Military	

Employment (Dates)	Occupation	Place	Employer

Religious Affiliation		Fraternal Affiliations	
Political Affiliation		Union Membership	

Organization Membership	
Racial, Ethnic, or Nationality Identification	
Principal Residence Locations Before Marriage (Include Dates)	
Principal Residence Locations After Marriage (Include Dates)	

Generations Chart
A Summary of Vital Data

This chart pulls together for quick reference
vital data on family members. Further details
on the individuals treated in the family history
should be developed on the other worksheets.

Father:

B:

M:

D:

**Writer's
Name:**

B:

M:

Spouse:

B:

M:

D:

Mother:

B:

M:

D:

Key
B: Birthplace and date
M: Marriage place and date
D: Place and date of death

Great-Grandfather:

B:

M:

D:

Great-Grandmother:

B:

M:

D:

Grandfather:

B:

M:

D:

Great-Grandfather:

B:

M:

D:

Great-Grandmother:

B:

M:

D:

Grandmother:

B:

M:

D:

Great-Grandfather:

B:

M:

D:

Great-Grandmother:

B:

M:

D:

Grandfather:

B:

M:

D:

Great-Grandfather:

B:

M:

D:

Great-Grandmother:

B:

M:

D:

Grandmother:

B:

M:

D: